Inspiration and Ideals

Thoughts for Every Day

Philippa Burgess

INSPIRATION AND IDEALS
Thoughts for Every Day

Philippa Burgess

This book was inspired by the book *Inspiration and Ideals, Thoughts for Every Day* by Grenville Kleiser (1917)

Copyright ©2016 All Rights Reserved

Disclaimer: The publisher and author make no representations of warranties.

Published in the United States by:

Inspiration & Ideals LLC
9975 Wadsworth Pkwy, Unit K2
Westminster, CO 80021
(720) 608-6201
www.InspirationandIdeals.com

Books may be purchased in quantity and/or special sales by contacting the publisher Inspiration and Ideals LLC through www.InspirationandIdeals.com or at Contact@InspirationandIdeals.com.

InspirationandIdeals.com
PhilippaBurgess.com

Publisher: Inspiration & Ideals LLC
Cover & Interior Design: Nick Zelinger (NZ Graphics)
Editing: Jeanne Stratton
Manuscript Consultation: Judith Briles (The Book Shepherd)
Marketing Group: Red Thread Creative Group
Independent Publisher Education: AuthorU.org
Author Photograph: Ashlee Bratton (Ashography)

ISBN 978-1-943724-01-7 (Hardcover)
ISBN 978-1-943724-00-0 (Paper)
ISBN 978-1-943724-02-4 (eBook)
Library of Congress Control Number: 2015912328

Categories for Cataloguing and Shelving
1) Spirituality 2) Inspirational 3) Philosophy

First Edition, Printed in U.S.A.

To Dr. Judith Briles, whose Kung Fu is better than mine
and who has helped beat books out of me that
I've been meaning to publish for years.

OTHER WORKS BY PHILIPPA BURGESS

BOOKS
Realize Your Big Screen Dream: The Guide for Authors to Bring Books to Film and Television (2016)

FILMS
Boulder Buddz (2017)

The Bridge You'll Never Cross

It's what you think that makes the world
Seem dull or bright to you;
Your mind may color all things gray
Or make them radiant hue.
Be glad today, be true and wise,
Seek gold amid the dross;
Waste neither time nor thought about
The bridge you'll never cross.

There's useful work for you to do
With hand and brain and heart;
There's urgent human service, too,
In which to take your part.
Make every opportunity
A gain and not a loss;
The best is yours, so do not fear
The bridge you'll never cross.

If life seems drab and difficult,
Just face it with a will;
You do not have to work alone
Since God is with you still.
Press on with courage toward the goal,
With Truth your shield emboss;
Be strong, look up and just ignore
The bridge you'll never cross.

– Grenville Kleiser

Preface

One summer as a child growing up in New Jersey, I found my original copy of *Inspiration and Ideals, Thoughts for Every Day* buried among other books in a tent at a flea market in Barnegat Light. It was a hardbound, faded, purple fabric-covered book with the title gold-embossed.

I was twelve years old at the time and had no idea what a gem I had acquired. Sometimes I would pick up old books, but often didn't find them to be all that interesting. This one was different. It pulled me in, and it has never let me go.

Everything in *Inspiration and Ideals* speaks to my beliefs, where the application of good thoughts and good efforts create a good life. Every time I revisit these words, it is like spending time with an old friend who offers both encouragement and wise counsel. The original author, Grenville Kleiser, reminded me, among many other truths, that "The eternal mind of God is consistently available to you. Go directly to God for your supply of good, and it will meet all your needs."

It was not my initial intention to publish this book. Rather, I was doing independent contracting and needed to come up with a name for an LLC. I founded Inspiration & Ideals, LLC. I started writing my first book, which has now become my second book, and somewhere along the line I brought new life to my now tattered copy of the original *Inspiration and Ideals*. It took on a life of its own as I continued to get a great amount of enthusiasm from my terrific team and community.

The first edition of *Inspiration and Ideals* was printed in 1910; the copy I still hold in my hands was the tenth reprint, published in 1917. I've read this book consistently though the years and have found its advice to be of value not only in my formative years, but throughout my life. I believe that if you were to judge a book by its cover, you might not have discovered the original; available copies of the original are rather tattered, are scanned from original print with numerous pen marks, or if in digital form, are mostly with scrunched-up copy.

What you now hold in your hands is designed to breathe new life into those words so they are not only remembered, but are accessible to today's reader. The philosophies in this book are designed to set a high bar for what is possible, what is true, what is good, and what is right. I hope you find it both vivifying and instructive in your own life's journey.

In designing the cover, I found the image of the butterfly fractal. It had the purple and gold I'd wanted to carry over from the original book cover. In showing it to some friends with an affinity for science, they commented on the fractal. I decided to expand upon that theme visually throughout the book. It speaks to our connection with nature and with the universe, and how there is a divine order to things that is available for us to see, meditate upon, and embrace in our own lives.

About Grenville Kleiser

Grenville Kleiser (1868-1935) was a North American author. He was born in 1868 in Toronto, Canada and married Elizabeth Thompson in 1894. Grenville died in August, 1935 in New York City. He was an author of inspirational books and guides to oratorical success and personal development. Kleiser also worked as an instructor in Public Speaking at Yale Divinity School, Yale University.

He dedicated the original book to his wife Elizabeth:

> TO ELIZABETH
> MY CONSTANT INSPIRATION,
> COUNSELLOR, AND IDEAL WIFE,
> THIS BOOK IS AFFECTIONATELY
> INSCRIBED

If you are interested in seeing the original work you may be able to find copies for sale on Amazon. These will be republished, scanned copies of an original book. Grenville Kleiser also wrote many other books; I encourage you to seek them out. If you would like to see any of them brought to new life, please don't hesitate to contact Inspiration & Ideals LLC.

His original endorsements read:

Every man keeps within himself an indestructible record of his own life.
– Hamilton Wright Mabie

Nothing relieves and ventilates the mind like a resolution.
– John Burroughs

Do you ask to be the companion of nobles? Make yourself noble, and you shall be. Do you long for the conversation of the wise? Learn to understand it, and you shall hear it.
– Ruskin

The ideal life is in our blood and never will be lost. Sad will be the day for any man when he becomes contented with the thoughts he is thinking and the deeds he is doing – where there is not forever beating at the doors of his soul some great desire to do something larger, which he knows he was meant and made to do.
– Phillips Brooks

Foreword

Thoughts rule mankind. Inspiration and aspiration must precede all great and enduring achievement. Ideals light the way to industry. Cheerfulness has a direct and beneficial influence upon health. Faith is the foundation of all large enterprise. Truth is the eternal quest of the human mind. Love is still the greatest thing in the world.

The purpose of this book is to give help and inspiration in right thinking and right living, and to suggest ideals which will make for material and spiritual welfare.

The author trusts that these thoughts, which he has found personally helpful, will stimulate and sustain many a fellow traveler on the journey along life's pathway.

Grenville Kleiser
New York City

JANUARY

JANUARY ONE

Priceless Time

Begin this day and year with clear purpose, strong resolve, and faith in your abilities.

Focus on the essentials.

Do your work well; the reward will be greater work and a larger sphere of usefulness.

Realize the priceless value of time and opportunity, and determine to make this day count toward the achievement of your goals.

JANUARY TWO

Universal Law

Healthy desires and aspirations bring increased happiness. When you begin the day with a fresh appetite for work and achievement, the world seems fresh and new.

Success and happiness result from following the path that resonates best with you.

Universal law is supreme, inexorable and eternal.

JANUARY THREE

To Do

To be strong and true;

To be generous in praise and appreciation of others;

To give without expectation of return;

To practice humility and tolerance;

To speak little and listen much;

To grow in grace, goodness, and gratitude;

To seek truth;

To work, love, pray, and serve daily;

This is to travel heavenward.

JANUARY FOUR

Great Purpose

When you have chosen a great purpose, concentrate on it.

Bend your best energies to it and guard yourself against subtle distractions.

Make it the focus of your daily life and be enthusiastic about it.

Substitute doing for dreaming, and achievement for wishing.

The great things of the world are done by those who specialize and focus.

JANUARY FIVE

Greatest Secret

I am the secret of health and happiness.

I am the inspiration of youth and the solace of age.

I am always available, invincible and eternal.

I am the healer of hatred and injustice.

I am the partner of truth.

I am the remedy for the world's wars, and woes.

I am the fulfillment of Universal law.

I am the greatest thing in the world.

I am Love.

JANUARY SIX

Valuable Goodwill

Goodwill is a valuable asset.

People around you are quick to read your attitudes toward them, which are communicated in ways other than words.

Goodwill is reciprocal; that which you send out to others will return to you multiplied.

Understand this, and people will be glad to know you.

JANUARY SEVEN

Universal Opposition

Good is constructive; Evil is destructive.

Good encourages, and sustains; Evil enslaves, and kills.

Good creates inspiring art; Evil darkens and blasts people's lives.

Good inspires faith and love; Evil produces dishonesty and hate.

Good is eternal.

JANUARY EIGHT

Broken Resolution

The remedy for a broken resolution is to recreate it, truer and stronger.

Renew and reiterate it.

If you have high ideals, you can act upon them if you choose firmness and perseverance.

Review each night what you have done during the day; clear-eyed self-examination is essential to progress.

JANUARY NINE

Clearest Thinking

Your clearest thinking can emerge from silence, solitude, and meditation.

When you relax deeply, you give your innermost power the opportunity to be revealed.

Beware the modern tendency to hurry and waste.

It is at times of inward stillness that you can most clearly rest in Divine presence.

JANUARY TEN

Quality Work

Whether your present work be great or small, the important thing is to do it well.

Good work confers benefits by enabling you to learn and grow.

However well or much you have already done, you can still do better and more.

Rise to the immense possibilities before you.

JANUARY ELEVEN

Eternal Truth

The more love you feel and express in your daily life, the more you are aligned with eternal truth.

Resolve this day to keep your thoughts in harmony with divine love, and the highest happiness will come to you.

God is good and God is everywhere, hence good is available to you always.

JANUARY TWELVE

A Thousand Doors

Education allows you greater opportunities for fulfillment, usefulness and happiness.

If each succeeding day finds you doing more, with increased joy and interest, then you are traveling in the right direction.

Life does not stand still.

Today a thousand doors are open to you.

Today is the day to achieve something worthwhile and to grow.

JANUARY THIRTEEN

Spiritual Knowing

The Universe supplies your heart with an inexhaustible stream of spiritual knowing.

As you apply this knowing in your daily life, you will become more deeply aware of your alignment with the source of all that is good, true and eternal.

When you seek guidance each day, and delight in following your heart, you will have a taste of heaven on earth.

JANUARY FOURTEEN

Constant Gratitude

Hold fast to the light; remember that this is invincible against the assaults of any misunderstanding or enemy.

Anchor your soul and you will stand steadfast through the storm.

Feel constant gratitude; this will strengthen and uphold you.

Let the spirit of truth guide you today and always.

JANUARY FIFTEEN

Harmonious Choices

The way to harmony, health and happiness is largely in your mind.

What you regularly choose to think about contributes significantly to your character and destiny.

There are many great minds in the world to stimulate and ennoble you.

Help, encouragement, healing and inspiration are readily available to you.

Choose them.

JANUARY SIXTEEN

Expectant Attitude

Keep your mind open to helpful suggestion.

Cultivate an expectant, hopeful attitude.

Emphasize the strong, uplifting elements of your nature.

Realize the value of faith and spiritual connection in living a life of vitality.

Cultivate confidence, quietness, and wholesomeness.

Constructive thinking is essential to health and happiness.

JANUARY SEVENTEEN

Clear Thinking

Daily meditation is an effective way to clear your thinking.

Great ideas are conceived and great projects planned through focus.

Daily mental training is essential to the enrichment of your life.

Intuition and aspiration are silent sculptors fashioning character and conduct.

Set aside time each day for quiet contemplation.

JANUARY EIGHTEEN

Constructive Behavior

When with other people, be a listener.

Be considerate in every word and act.

Cultivate tolerance.

Do not speak of yourself unnecessarily, and do not speak ill of another.

Be aware of the tone and temper of your conversation.

Be very slow to pass judgment; examine and judge yourself rather than others.

JANUARY NINETEEN

Self-Respect

Let your work speak for itself; do your best, and let the world make its own appraisal.

Cultivate a sense of independence that will carry you in the middle of a crowd as well as in solitude.

Shun doing in secret what you would not do openly.

Let your priority be to merit your own respect, and it will follow that you will have the respect of others.

JANUARY TWENTY

Unique Gifts

Deep in every human soul is a longing to do something good and enduring, to use your gifts to contribute to a larger purpose.

As you listen to this inner voice, you will discover your own strengths, which can help you to fulfill your purpose.

It is your choice and responsibility to use these unique gifts.

JANUARY TWENTY-ONE

Intelligent Optimism

Think optimistically and constructively.

If you encounter difficulty, take a brisk walk and breathe deeply.

Look for the best things in life, and resolve to be an intelligent optimist.

Now is the time to take Universal truth as it is offered to you, and to use it for your immediate growth and advancement.

JANUARY TWENTY-TWO

Superfluous Possessions

Material possessions that you do not need and cannot use may only encumber you.

Regularly examine what you have and get rid of what you don't really want.

Choose things that express your own individuality.

Look for quality rather than quantity. Excess is wasteful.

Don't burden yourself with the superfluous.

JANUARY TWENTY-THREE

Personal Growth

Culture is personal growth, not accumulation of things. It is enlightenment acquired through experience.

Culture has to do with quality, not quantity; it is never loud, boastful, conspicuous, or self-assertive.

It expresses itself in poise, gentleness, considerateness, and self-control.

True culture makes for fullness and freedom of life.

JANUARY TWENTY-FOUR

Within You

True happiness depends upon close alignment with the Universe.

The delusion of accolades, the emptiness of riches and the stupidity of selfishness are manifest on all sides.

All the enjoyment that the world can provide is nothing compared with the priceless riches which are derived from close daily communion with that which is within you.

JANUARY TWENTY-FIVE

Positive Focus

One of the secrets to a happy life is to focus on your likes and to ignore your dislikes.

If your mind tends to criticism, fault-finding, and disapproval, it will readily find exactly that every hour of the day.

As you dwell upon the best aspects of life, you will find your own life becoming happier, better, and more productive.

JANUARY TWENTY-SIX

Appreciated Achievement

That which comes without effort may not be adequately appreciated.

Blessed, therefore, is the one who plans, toils, perseveres, faces disappointments and surmounts obstacles.

There is nothing that can quite take the place of personal effort and hard-won achievement.

JANUARY TWENTY-SEVEN

Spiritual Foundation

Sooner or later you must discover your spiritual foundation to have true happiness.

Confidence and stability rest upon truth.

God ever speaks to a receptive mind.

Knowledge of spiritual truth will give you a grateful sense of the joy of living.

Keep yourself in tune with the infinite, and harmony and happiness will be yours.

JANUARY TWENTY-EIGHT

Productive Thinking

Keep your mind filled with strong, productive thinking.

Begin each day with a clear mental picture of what you most desire to accomplish, and then earnestly work to that end.

Waste no time on antagonism.

Think mainly of practical things.

Constructive interests and activities will keep you happy.

Substitute doing for procrastination.

JANUARY TWENTY-NINE

Deep Breathing

Devote some time daily to deep breathing exercise, ideally outdoors.

As you walk, inhale deeply, expand the abdomen, and exhale fully.

Many people use only the upper part of the lungs in breathing.

Deep breathing should be practiced daily until it becomes an unconscious habit.

This is absolutely essential to good health.

JANUARY THIRTY

Mental Hygiene

Whatever your present situation may be, you can perform a seeming miracle by changing your thoughts.

Your thought world is a sacred place.

It is always with you and is exclusively yours.

Nothing can invade it without your consent.

Keep your mental kingdom clean and you will be whole.

JANUARY THIRTY-ONE

Patient Persistence

The gift of patient persistence is akin to genius.

To be able to work and wait, knowing that results will inevitably follow your efforts, is a sign of wisdom.

Life is a great school for study, experimentation, observation, enterprise, and achievement.

Your mental abilities are as real a possession to you as money, land, or other material property.

FEBRUARY

FEBRUARY ONE

Happiness is a Mental Habit

There are two kinds of optimists – wise, and otherwise. The intelligent optimist not only believes things will be right, but works diligently to make them so. He thinks everything is ordered for the best, that the world tends inevitably toward the good, the true and the beautiful.

The disposition of the optimist to look only for the best in life gives him increased advantage in finding what he is looking for.

Happiness is a habit, not a locality. Optimism is intimately bound up with great achievement.
The true optimist gets the most out of life for himself, while augmenting the faith and courage of his associates.

Intelligent optimism will make one an enthusiast, and enthusiasm is the driving force in all great enterprise.

FEBRUARY TWO

The Kingdom of God is Within You

You have been created to be good, healthy, happy and prosperous. You have within your consciousness all the requisites for present and eternal happiness.

You possess within yourself all the power necessary for great usefulness and enduring achievement. You are made in the perfect likeness of God, who is Mind, Spirit, Life, Love and Truth.

Fully realize and apply the truth of your divine heritage, and you will be free from evil, sickness, discord, and everything unlike good. Fill your mind completely and constantly with thoughts of purity, faith, love and righteousness.

Seek first to know the Kingdom of God, and health, harmony, and happiness will be added unto you, for the Kingdom of God is within you.

FEBRUARY THREE

Influence People by Your Example

Eliminate resistance and resentment from your mind. Know them as subtle mental poisons. If things go wrong, look first for the cause in yourself.

Be quick to acknowledge in yourself your own shortcomings, and make haste to correct them.

Take time to improve your own nature, and seek to influence other people by your example rather than your criticism. In the face of unjust opposition, violent argument, or personal abuse, hold yourself in poise, knowing that truth is infallible.

A genial temper, broad charity, and quiet equanimity, under all circumstances, will give you mastery of yourself and the situation.

The silent and unconscious example of high thinking will do more on your part to help others than words and counsel.

FEBRUARY FOUR

Cultivate Gentleness and Courtesy

There is special need for gentle manners and courtesy in the home. The familiarity of family in intercourse may unconsciously lead to laxity in kindness, willingness, and considerateness.

Habits of self-restraint, intelligent tact, and self-sacrifice are frequently needed where people of varied tastes and temperaments are in intimate daily contact. It is remarkable what one member of a household can do by means of right personal example.

When you apply the qualities of sincerity, graciousness, courtesy, cheerfulness and affectionate regard toward those in your family circle, you have set in motion an influence which cannot be adequately estimated.

Love always wins, and it is still the greatest thing in the world.

FEBRUARY FIVE

Your Rightful Place in the World

Your present and future welfare depends mainly upon yourself. Do not look outside for help. Do not assume that the influence of others on your behalf would enable you to do better or accomplish more.

Realize you have within yourself all the power, ability, energy, and resources for building a highly successful life.

There is one great gift which is distinctly your own, and it is your profound duty to discover, develop and use it. The vital thing is not whether you have many talents, but the practical use you are making of your one great talent.

Let this inspiring thought give strength to your will and purpose to your daily work, and ultimately lead you to your rightful place in the world.

FEBRUARY SIX

You Have Unlimited Resources

Do not over-plan, nor be unduly anxious. Submit all to God and obey his guiding voice implicitly. Let the prayer, "Thy will be done," be a true petition of your heart.

The fruit of the spirit is joy, peace, long-suffering, gentleness, goodness, faith, meekness, temperance: against such there is no law.

From this sublime statement is the obvious that as you cultivate and express these qualities in your daily life, you will be close to God and free from the possibility of condemnation.

Worry is a form of weakness, tacit acknowledgment of self-limitation and lack of confidence. To live a large life, you must have large stores of personal courage.

The realization that you have unlimited resources will fortify you for the more formidable enterprises.

FEBRUARY SEVEN

Prize the Quick-Passing Moments

O the waste of golden moments! Throngs of men and woman drifting hither and thither, aiming at nothing, going nowhere. See the crowds of restless, uncertain, wandering people – great unceasing procession of tired and disappointed humanity. As for you, be well advised and fill your daily life with definite purpose.

Know where you are going, what you wish to attain, and the precise means you are using to reach the desired goal.

Make use of the valuable moments so prodigally wasted by the unthinking. Realize how well-spent minutes multiply into hours of productive effort.

Prize the quick passing moments for their personal value. You have all the time there is, and now is the opportune time to do the best that is in you.

FEBRUARY EIGHT

Make Your Thoughts Work for You

Put your principles into practice. What you do, not what you say, is the essential thing.

Stimulate your sluggish ideas and ideals into action. Dormant aspirations are of value only as they are translated into acts.

Make your best thoughts work for you. Transform your desires into deeds, your resolutions into results. Your personal powers are made up chiefly of principles, ideals, desires, and resolutions. The specific way in which you use these powers in your daily life largely determines your degree of success.

Give earnest attention to these vital things; apply them intelligently, and you will go forward to inevitable achievement.

Success will be yours precisely in the degree that you use your powers aright.

FEBRUARY NINE

Make Your Daily Life Constructive

Let your daily self-examination be searching and severe. If you are subject to such faults as anger, passion, impulsiveness, or resentment, examine each of them separately and formulate definite ways to overcome them.

At the close of each day submit yourself to a rigid self-examination to detect such faults. This review of the day should be thorough and deliberate. Know precisely what high motives you have disregarded, what good resolutions you have broken, what admonitions of conscience you have stifled.

Acknowledgement and confession are true means of spiritual attainment. Be quite sure that your life is positive, constructive, and purposeful.

Make it your earnest aim to do something daily which you can measure in tangible results.

FEBRUARY TEN

Dedicate Yourself to High Ideals

Dedicate your life to the service of God. You can carry this lofty spirit into all of your daily activities, wherever their nature may be. If it is well to serve God at any time, then it is well to serve Him at all times.

If you should use one of your gifts for the honor of God, then you should use all of your gifts for this great purpose.

If it is desirable that you should practice purity, wisdom and righteousness some of the time, surely it is equally desirable that you practice these great virtues all of the time.

There can be no higher purpose in your life than to serve God at all times, in every thought, word and act. It is your privilege to do this from this day forth.

God waits on your answer. Think on these things.

FEBRUARY ELEVEN

Press on to Worthy Achievement

Your speech and manner proclaim you. Be judicious in your choice of words. Make the most of your powers and abilities.

Let your thought be uniformly deep, dignified, and deliberate, so that these qualities may unconsciously manifest themselves in your outward manner.

Have a proper sense of self-respect, and show it in your voice, speech, and personality. There will never be a better time than the present to make the most of yourself and to initiate plans for a larger life.

Go forward with new purpose, confident of ultimate success. Launch your best powers now, without further delay, knowing that earnest and diligent effort will surely bring adequate reward.

Look away to the heights, and press on to worthy achievement.

FEBRUARY TWELVE

Daily Progress in Self-Culture

Let these questions stimulate you to the highest effort: What is the best way for me to spend the hours of each day? To what particular purpose should I devote my chief efforts?

How can I make the most of my life? In what ways can I improve my daily opportunities? How can I make greater progress than I am now doing?

What is the highest aim I can set for myself as a life ambition? How can I be quite sure that I am working with right methods toward right ends? How can I best advance each day in personal culture, mental power, and righteousness?

What is the most practical and immediate way for me to build my life for large usefulness and service?

What particular ways shall I wish that I had taken, when I am leaving the world?

FEBRUARY THIRTEEN

Opportunities for Your Abilities

Apply great abilities to small things and the results will be small. Apply small abilities to great things and the results will be better. But apply great abilities to great things and the results will be great. This is the key to large success. If you now feel discontented or circumscribed, plan to change gradually to a better and bigger place.

There is no valid reason why you should struggle along indefinitely in a wrong vocation or an uncongenial atmosphere. The world offers wide and varied opportunities for your abilities.

Be quick to realize and correct your shortcomings. To remain ignorant of your defects is to defraud yourself.

You were made to progress, to grow in power and influence, and to achieve some great and worthy purpose.

FEBRUARY FOURTEEN

Always Give Your Best to Others

Criticism should be suggestive, not arbitrary. Insistent advice may repel rather than help. Personal example is more influential than many words. Criticism and advice too freely given is rarely appreciated.

A wise reticence is a safeguard against many blunders. It is better to say too little than too much. When you look for the best you will see little of the worst. It will keep you tolerably busy to keep your own life in order and to conform it to a great standard.

The good you think about other people influences them unconsciously, even though you do not express it in words. The purpose of your criticism should always be to help and encourage.

Give your best to others, and they will ultimately give their best to you.

FEBRUARY FIFTEEN

Walking for Health and Vigor

Walking is one of the best forms of exercise. It confers physical, mental and spiritual benefits. The correct way to walk is to carry the chest high, chin level, and throw the legs energetically out from the thigh.

Right walking puts a tingle in the blood, promotes digestion, clarifies the mind, and elevates the spirit. If you walk alone, charge your mind with lofty subjects, such as your intimate alliance with the source of all power.

If you walk with a companion, talk upon something of mutual interest and helpfulness. Energetic walking stimulates unsuspected thoughts into action.

Walk enough every day, with energetic stride, deep breathing, and definite purpose, and it will contribute to your health and longevity.

FEBRUARY SIXTEEN

Right Desire is True Prayer

The chief purpose of your prayer is not to instruct God, but to bring yourself into harmony with Him. Prayer is not to multiply material possessions, not to satisfy selfish desires. You pray to God for guidance and protection.

As you make your mind receptive, God's spiritual ideas pour into it in full and satisfying measure.

The good thus sent to you in unlimited supply meets a deep need of your nature, and gradually you come to realize that true prayer is right desire and that such prayer is always answered.

Earnestness of desire is better than multiplied words.

True prayer promotes humility, patience, self-denial, peace and gentleness.

The final test of true prayer is that it confers upon you increased joy, faith, and courage.

FEBRUARY SEVENTEEN

Go Forward with Unflinching Will

There are occasions when you must will strongly and decisively if you would achieve. To believe yourself able and efficient is a prerequisite to large accomplishment.

The happiness and prosperity of many men have been due largely to courage and confidence, based upon well-established habits of decision, purpose, and constancy.

The activities, duties, and problems of your daily life will be likely to make severe demands upon you, but you will be equal to every demand if your character is solidly founded upon principle.

The ability to make sound decisions, and to put them promptly into execution, has been a lead characteristic of distinguished men.

Be sure to choose your course wisely, then go forward with unflinching will.

FEBRUARY EIGHTEEN

Put Forth Your Best Effort Now

A serious problem is to know what to do when you are confronted by dark and discouraging days. The sun seems effaced. You are in deep despair and depression. Your heart is heavy. You are mastered by material misfortune. You feel perturbed, pessimistic, powerless.

But the solution for this seemingly sad condition is at your ready hand. The remedy lies in hard work. Apply yourself at once to an earnest, energetic, mind-absorbing task, and your troubles will rapidly take wing.

Do this with faith, and believe that the remedy and reward will be speedy and sure.

Life is short, hence the importance of putting forth your best effort today.

Work has the mark of divine approbation, since happiness is conferred not upon idleness but upon labor.

FEBRUARY NINETEEN

Study Great and Inspiring Words

The study of words is a delightful and beneficial occupation. Frequently meditate upon words which express great ideas.

Select one such word at a time, and try to realize fully its beauty, meaning, and significance.

Take the word "truth" and carefully consider its value and importance. Think of its universal application. Study it thoroughly until you have made it your own.

In like manner, study such great words as "immortality," "justice," "love," "God," "hero," "faith," "sublimity," "heaven," "righteousness," "world," "leadership," "power," "humility," "beauty," "wisdom," "perfection," "friendship," and "prosperity."

As you deeply meditate upon such words, you will be conscious of mental uplift and expansion.

FEBRUARY TWENTY

Cultivate Power of Concentration

Concentration is a great distinguishing faculty of men of high purpose. The ability to apply your mind steadily and exclusively to one subject at a time is a mark of superior power and essential to really great achievement.

Concentration can be cultivated by regular and conscientious practice. When you detect your mind wandering, instantly substitute the desired subject for the intrusive one. Repeated efforts of this kind will rapidly remedy the fault.

Be on your guard against mind-wandering and idle day-dreaming as enemies of culture and progress.

Be deeply interested in what you are doing, and ignore vagrant ideas. Concentration will rapidly build your mental power. It is vital to large mental growth and personal advancement.

FEBRUARY TWENTY-ONE

Do Things Deliberately and Calmly

Men who hurry most, accomplish least. When your plan has been well made, you can proceed to the day's duties with deliberateness and confidence.

Your best and deepest thoughts will disclose themselves at times of stillness, not in a blustering tempest of over-activity.

Moreover, a uniformly tranquil spirit will safeguard you against many common mistakes of judgment and feeling.

As you form the habit of doing everything deliberately and calmly, you will accomplish more, do it better, and have the satisfaction at the close of the day of having used your powers to the largest advantage.

Thus work will become to you an increasing pleasure, leading you to constantly higher accomplishment.

FEBRUARY TWENTY-TWO

The Lessons of Daily Experience

Experience is the great school master of life, constantly disciplining you through tests, trials, and difficulties. It imposes penalties for mistakes and misjudgments. It indicates where danger lies, and warns you of inevitable punishment lurking in undesirable directions.

Thus you learn the penalty for waste of time, the scattering of energies, the pursuit of ill-considered plans, and the prodigal squandering of physical and mental power.

Experience tells you not to repeat an offense lest greater punishment befall you.

Experience makes you understand that you are living in a real world, with real work to do, and serious problems to solve.

Carefully note the lessons of daily experience, that your life may be rounded out into fullness.

FEBRUARY TWENTY-THREE

How to Meet Daily Demands

There are inevitable interruptions in every busy life. When you have planned to do a special piece of work, there will be a visitor, a telephone call, or some other inopportune demand made upon your time. Then will be put to the test your degree of courtesy, good-humor, and unselfishness.

However diligent and methodical you may be in allotting your work hours, you should allow for the trivialities that are an unavoidable part of daily life.

Submit gracefully to unforeseen interruptions, and use them as opportunities for growth in patience, adaptability and kindness.

A compulsory distraction may be a blessing in disguise, after which you can return to your routine work refreshed and elevated.

FEBRUARY TWENTY-FOUR

Look to the Quality of Your Work

Place special emphasis upon the quality of your work. When the chief aim of your daily life is to produce intrinsically the best, and not merely the outwardly attractive, you can then afford to disregard the approval and praise of men.

The inner consciousness of work worthily attempted and well done is its own reward. Let your thoughts be of quality, not quantity.

To do good work you must be interested in it, and to be interested in it you must like it. All the master builders have been earnest, intense, conscientious workers.

You can be one of the great men of the world, in the degree that you put quality into your daily work, seeking always for results rather than approbation.

Your opportunities are unlimited.

FEBRUARY TWENTY-FIVE

Submit Your Will to that of God

The highest purpose of your life is to do God's will. There is nothing greater than this. It transcends all other duties. Men are haunted by the possibilities of the ideal life; they feel a yearning for spiritual perfection.

Every thinking man turns at last to God and asks for guidance. He wants to know God's will that he may fulfill the expectations of the all-wise Father.

The first vital step toward spiritual realization is to submit your will to that of God, to surrender freely and wholly to Him, and to listen attentively and obediently to His guiding voice.

You may search the wide world over for happiness, but you will not find it in its completeness until you have made the great self-surrender to God.

FEBRUARY TWENTY-SIX

Do Something Fine and Noble Today

There is something sublime about the beginning of a new day. Perhaps the previous night has been filled with dark misgivings, disappointments, and oppressive fears.

But the fresh beginning of a new day, with its beautiful light and promise of unexplored possibilities, should gladden the heart and inspire the soul.

Look upward at the beginning of the day. This simple act will elevate your mind and impel you to go forth with new confidence and power.

A day is well-lived in which you have put a fine resolution into practice, achieved a definite purpose, done some worthy act of kindness, or rendered a noble service to others.

True service is not limited to time or place. Today is the day to do something fine and noble.

FEBRUARY TWENTY-SEVEN

Conversation and Self-Discipline

Conversation is a form of self-revelation. There you unconsciously disclose your merits and defects, your virtues and idiosyncrasies. The very freedom of conversation takes you off your guard, and exposes you to the scrutiny of others. Hence the importance of speech culture.

Study your manner and method of speaking. Train your voice in the qualities of purity, resonance, and power. Enunciate distinctly, and pronounce accurately.

Choose your words with fastidious care. Endeavor constantly to improve your style of speaking, and make each occasion of speech an opportunity for self-discipline.

Give preference to pleasant, helpful, interesting subjects. Use your daily conversation as a means to self-culture and personal progress.

FEBRUARY TWENTY-EIGHT

Have a Set of Ruling Motives

When you can truthfully say that God is the light and strength of your life, and that you consciously depend upon Him every hour of the day, you will fear no man. Trust Him absolutely and you will be kept in perfect peace.

The truth of God is more to be coveted than the finest gold. The divine promise is that if you hunger after righteousness you will be satisfied.

Have a set of ruling motives for daily living. Constantly aim at a higher and better quality of thought.

An infinite supply of truth is now at your service, to choose in what measure you will. A great heritage of spiritual riches is yours merely for the taking and using.

Claim what is yours today, and let your life express the truth, love, and goodness of the eternal Mind.

FEBRUARY TWENTY-NINE

Do What You Ought to Do Today

Be grateful today for opportunity to work and serve. Keep a definite purpose before you, and bend to its accomplishment your best abilities.

Put the strength of your mind and muscle into the urgent duty of the moment, that it may be done well.

Good work is a divine provision for developing your initiative, self-reliance, diligence, and other sterling qualities. Do what you ought to do in a true spirit of gladness and gratitude.

Make the fresh beginning of this day an occasion for stronger resolutions. Let the close of the day witness to your new acquisitions, graces, and accomplishments.

To you belongs today, with its estimable opportunities for work, achievement, and human helpfulness.

MARCH

MARCH ONE

Happiness is a Mental Habit

Spiritual health is the basis of physical health. Lofty thoughts, high ideals, and worthy ambitions stimulate and inspire the mind, and thence react upon the body imparting to it purity, sweetness, soundness and vigor. A devoted love to God, and an earnest desire to know and obey His precepts, inevitably gives new power to the mind.

The efficacy of a single spiritual thought, in promoting health of mind and vigor of body, cannot be over-estimated.

Careless, indifferent, impure thoughts are perilous, and sometimes fatal.

Let your thoughts, ambitions, and ideals be wholly drawn from God's infinite supply, and your life will be wholesome, happy, healthy, and beautiful. Think clean, healthy, constructive thoughts, and your body will be correspondingly strong and well.

MARCH TWO

Will to Do Right Yourself

Cultivate flexibility of mind. Resist the tendency to want things always your way, and to have other people necessarily conform their lives to your ideas. Good reasons unknown to you may be guiding them ultimately to the best results. Life would be monotonous if all people thoughts and acted precisely alike.

Diversity of thought and purpose are essential to a progressive world.

Will to do right yourself, but do not use your will to control and dominate others. The habit of generous acquiescence gives right balance to a strong-willed nature. You may have the will-power of a giant, but you should not misuse it.

Be kind, generous, and forgiving, since these are qualities which link you closely to God.

MARCH THREE

The Product of Repeated Choice

You have inspired moments, times of mental exaltation, when you feel a sense of unlimited personal power. This is the time to note such thoughts, and to set them down in writing for actual use. Make a record of your new ideas, plans, purposes, ideals, and resolutions.

The habit of putting these vital matters into writing will make them more definite and concrete, and serve to remind you of possible negligence.

Bear in mind that there is not a moment in which your character is not being shaped in one direction or another, and that your life is simply the product of repeated choices.

Grandeur of character is the effect of many habits. Know precisely what you want, proceed directly to it, and the best results will reward your diligence.

MARCH FOUR

Common Sense Habits of Eating

Masticate your food thoroughly. The vital thing in eating is what you assimilate. Avoid the common fault of bolting food. If in a hurry, eat less and masticate more. Thoroughly chewing food not only makes it more palatable, but is a valuable aid to digestion.

Be discriminating in your choice of food. Eat for health. Plain, well-cooked food is much more nourishing than over-variety. If a food disagrees with you, give it up. Eat plentifully of fresh vegetables and fruits.

Relish your food, but never eat to satiety. Most persons eat too much.

Quantity and kind of food should be determined by the nature of your daily work and activities.

Keep your wants few and simple, and eat only food that agrees with you.

MARCH FIVE

Make This Personal Pledge Today

Personal pledge: I hereby solemnly promise that, from this day forth, I will endeavor to make the best use of my time, ability and energy. I will promptly correct in myself every undesirable habit.

I will diligently aim to make daily progress toward truth and perfection. I will keep my thought upon a high plane of worthy effort.

I will make the most of my present opportunities as the best means of fitting myself for larger responsibilities. I will think and act according to the dictates of my conscious.

I will try sincerely to render helpful service to others. I will cultivate intelligent optimism, self-confidence, dignity, and independence.

I will so spend each day, that at night I can lie down with assurance of God's love and approbation.

MARCH SIX

The Eternal Supremacy of Good

Your mental attitude is a great determining influence in your daily life. Begin the day with an expectant and energetic mental attitude toward your work, plans, and purposes, and it will elevate and enhance all your activities.

The spirit in which you regard your fellow men and the world about you will be reflected back to you.

When you are in the right mental attitude, many things will seem to conspire and cooperate to advance your work and interests.

Primarily it is your mental attitude which makes the day happy and productive, or the contrary.

You can demonstrate the truth of this today by resolving to look only for the best, to be intelligently optimistic, and to have confidence in the eternal supremacy of good.

MARCH SEVEN

Put Your Ideas into Practice

Make more positive resolutions regarding the things you ought to do. Bring every available reinforcement to bear upon your resolutions.

Write down on a card the special things you resolve to do, and read it several times a day. Repeat it aloud at frequent intervals. Assert in vigorous tones of voice the thoughts you wish to establish as unconscious habits in your life.

The best means of impressing new resolutions upon your mind is by concentration, iteration, and vigorous assertion.

At the close of every day review your thoughts and actions, and know precisely what you have done with your new resolutions.

It is a great thing to conceive a great idea, but it is still greater to put it into execution.

MARCH EIGHT

The Practical Value of Meditation

A profitable pastime is to select a significant saying, and meditate upon it for a few minutes until you have made it your own. By this simple means you can furnish your mind with many beautiful and inspiring thoughts, which will be ready to serve you at times of need.

The following thoughts will be of suggestive value in this respect: God is love. True knowledge is based on truth. Divine Mind is eternal. Right thinking is prayer. Truth, good, and beauty should each be sought for its own sake.

Faith is always creative. Thrift of time brings ripeness of mind. Opinion of good men is but knowledge in the making.

Books are the bloodless substitute for life. We live in an ascending scale when we live happily.

An inspiration is a joy forever.

MARCH NINE

Constructive Thoughts and Ideals

It is better to talk of health, progress, happiness, and success, than of the contrary things. It is better to think of the beautiful, truthful, inspiring, and ideal, than the opposite thoughts.

It is better to be cheerful, confident, expectant, and enthusiastic than to indulge in destructive feelings.

Knowing this, the right course is clearly open to you. Fill your daily life so full of constructive thoughts and ideals, that there will be no room for negative and depressing ideas.

Confine your conversation to helpful, useful, encouraging subjects. Be generous in thought, word, act, and purpose.

Make the world better for your being in it. Take a strong stand for truth and righteousness, and make every day count toward your eternal progress and happiness.

MARCH TEN

You Have a Great Heritage

You may read many good books, hear much wise counsel, and make emphatic personal resolutions, but until you have the Spirit of God consciously active in your daily life you will not reach true greatness.

It is well to store your mind with right and lofty truths, tho their real value to you depends upon the practical use you make of them.

Apply the truth which you now possess, and still greater truth will be revealed to you. The highest standard is not too high for you to choose as your constant guide.

God's ways are higher than your ways, and He is constantly pouring forth His inexhaustible supply of perfect ideas, which are yours for the mere taking and using.

You have a great and goodly heritage, but you must claim it for yourself.

MARCH ELEVEN

Serve God With a Willing Mind

Be strong and work. Whatsoever thy hand findeth to do, do it with thy might. God shall bring every work into judgment.

Establish yourself in every good word and work. Labor not for the meat which perisheth, but for that meat which the Son of Man shall give unto you.

Do justly, love mercy, and walk humbly with thy God. Add to your faith virtue; and to virtue knowledge; and to knowledge temperance; and to temperance patience; and to patience Godliness; and to Godliness brotherly kindness; and to brotherly kindness charity.

Seek first the Kingdom of God, and His righteousness, and all these things shall be added unto you.

The God of hope fills you with all joy and peace in believing. Serve Him with a perfect heart, and with a willing mind.

MARCH TWELVE

The Product of Right Thinking

Sincerity, kindness, and trust-worthiness often carry a man to honorable success more rapidly and surely than the possession of brilliant talents.

It is inspiring to observe how some men have marched steadily forward toward large achievement, not because of conspicuous ability, but as a result of patient, definite, and conscientious effort.

Hence it is that some men of great promise accomplish so little, while others who are quiet, unostentatious, self-possessed, and diligent, achieve astonishing results.

The world has placed a high valuation upon certain cardinal qualities of character, and he who possesses these in fullest degree will ultimately be most highly honored.

Right character is the product of right thoughts.

MARCH THIRTEEN

Make Your Resolution Emphatic

You are aware of having made many resolutions which you have not fully put into execution. Recognizing their importance and desirability, you intended to make them a working force in your life, but as time passed they were pushed aside, neglected, or forgotten.

The obvious conclusion from this common experience is that if you really want your resolutions to become active and significant forces in your life, you must adopt special means to this end.

Scrutinize your weaknesses and shortcomings and see precisely wherein you have failed.

Make your resolutions more emphatic, and keep strict account of what you do with them.

Determine with all your power to make them concrete in your daily activities.

MARCH FOURTEEN

Goodness is a Force of Attraction

Good attracts good. The man of upright character radiates an influence for good wherever he goes. Goodness of mind reflects itself in the face and manner so that it can be clearly read by other men.

A genuinely good man is a constant guide and inspiration to those about him. It is amazing what the personal example of a good man will do in imparting confidence, vitality, and enthusiasm to his friends and associates.

A virtuous life is often more persuasively eloquent than much verbal counsel.

It is well to mingle freely with good men, that their influence and example may be felt and utilized, but it is still better to be a good man.

Goodness has a power all its own to instruct, persuade, and inspire.

MARCH FIFTEEN

Your Immense Powers and Resources

This day brings to you its share of duties, opportunities, and responsibilities. The spirit in which you approach the work and activities of this new day will vitally affect the results.

Go forward with large confidence and high expectation.

Be faithful to your obligations, and discharge every duty with promptitude and thoroughness. Be alert to the fresh opportunities of this day, and do everything possible to advance your highest and best interests.

Stimulate your mind with clear, strong, uplifting ideas of what you wish to accomplish, and realize the immense powers and resources at your personal command.

Make this day mark a distinct and important advance in your progress toward a great ideal life.

MARCH SIXTEEN

How You Should Speak in Public

When you speak in public be thoroughly prepared, begin slowly, speak distinctly, proceed logically, and end promptly.

Be modest, direct, conversational, sincere, earnest, and uniformly courteous. Observe your pauses, suit the action to the word, look your audience in the eyes, and make yourself interesting.

Speak deliberately, be yourself at your best, keep to your subject and the facts. Favor the deep tones of your voice, and breathe from the abdomen.

Depend upon the sincerity of your effort to drive your thought home. Maintain an attitude of uniform mental poise. Lead your audience to a high level of thought and purpose.

Let the truth and intensity of your message carry conviction and persuasion to your hearers.

MARCH SEVENTEEN

Live Today a Full-Orbed Life

Let your life be broad, sympathetic, lofty, and comprehensive. Beware those habits and ruts which unconsciously limit men who are too much absorbed in single pursuits.

Keep the windows of your mind wide open to the light from all directions. Give your spirit a daily flight of exercise and freedom. Let the innermost thoughts of your mind gain strength and significance through expression.

Liberate the fine feelings of love, joyousness, enthusiasm, nobility, gratitude, and appreciation, that your heart may expand into fullness.

Live now a full-orbed life. It is better to be good-natured than great. To be sincerely beloved by your friends and associates transcends all material riches.

Live your largest life today.

MARCH EIGHTEEN

Discriminate in Your Use of Words

You think in words – with words you talk, command, appeal, convince, persuade. Study words so that you can use them significantly, effectively, worthily. Study them in your dictionary and in the works of standard writers.

Be discriminating in your use of words.

Make lists of the best words and incorporate them in your daily speech.

Begin with a list like this: Extenuate, revere, beguile, poignant, admirable, trenchant, umbrage, incredulity, facetious, sequestered, vagary, fidelity, obliquity, radiance, fantastic, ubiquitous, dissent, rectitude, duplicity, illustrious, fragile, chronicle, voracious, meticulous, scrupulous, lucid, venerate, aversion, ingenuous.

Daily study of words is a delightful and profitable pastime.

MARCH NINETEEN

You Have All the Time There Is

Every thinking man comes to realize how rapidly time passes. When the realization of this fully dawns upon him, his inclination is to hurry in the desire to attempt to achieve more.

Here, however, it is well for him to ponder the situation deeply and deliberately. He should realize that he really has at his disposal all the time there is, and that the important thing is to know how to formulate the best plans for securing the desired results.

When this is done with prudence and judgment, he can proceed with his appointed work with the assurance that his plans have been well made.

Under these circumstances he should have no thought of haste, but do all with a sense of personal power and confidence.

MARCH TWENTY

The Promise of Golden Days

The unfolding time of spring brings new hope and courage to man-kind. Nature gradually assumes her garb of warmth, tenderness, and freshness. The sunshine searches out the hidden places of earth, and repeats her miracle of making the world a smiling flower garden.

Spring comes softly and gently to smooth away the rough lines of winter, filling the air with perfume and melody, and awakening things to life. It is the promise of golden days and lingering lights.

It is the time of graceful transformation, when the secrets of nature are slowly revealed to the wondering senses. Birds and blossoms, leaves and flowers, trees and mountains, give ever-increasing delight, and all nature seems to join as in one great choral song of praise and gratitude.

MARCH TWENTY-ONE

The Secret of True Friendship

True friendship is not based upon selfish bargaining. It makes no undue demands, is not super-sensitive, gives without thought of return, and generously overlooks faults.

It is careful not to offend, and is tactful and discriminating when shadows of doubt appear.

True friendship expresses itself in interest, sympathy, good-will, and affection. It is free from self-consciousness and self-assertiveness. It is always ready to listen and to serve. If you are to have a true friend, first be one.

Diligently cultivate within yourself the rare qualities which comprise such a friendship.

In the degree that you are ready to give, serve, sympathize, and help, with no thought of return or reward, in such degree will you build sweet and enduring friendships.

MARCH TWENTY-TWO

Take Your Rightful High Place

There is more sympathy, sincerity, and spirit of sacrifice in the world than ever before. Many men have come to realize the power and desirability of kindness, unselfishness, and integrity.

In business and social life these and similar qualities are being applied with constantly increasing success.

The world is gradually becoming better, largely because of the self-denial, heroism, and nobility of thousands of men and women.

The world is steadily growing more interesting, beautiful, and inspiring, chiefly because of these consecrated lives.

It is your privilege and opportunity to take a place in this brotherhood of earnest and willing workers, and thereby to contribute your share to the world's betterment.

MARCH TWENTY-THREE

The Useful Practice of Writing

Form the valuable habit of writing down important thoughts which you wish to have prominently before your mind.

The note-books which you keep in this way, compromising significant ideas from your own mind and from the books you read, will become valuable repositories of truth.

The practice of writing will impress such thoughts clearly upon your mind, and reading them aloud at intervals will tend to make the impressions indelible.

Vague and vagrant thoughts are clarified and improved in the process of putting them into written form.

Ideas are not fully your own until you have expressed them clearly in speech and writing. The note-book habit is of immense practical value in training the mind to clear and logical thinking.

MARCH TWENTY-FOUR

Develop a Forceful Personality

Personality plays a vital part in building a successful career. The man of pleasing and forceful personality readily attracts and keeps friends.

His services are in constant demand. He is a power in business, a favorite in society, and in public life the man of the hour.

An important element in a strong personality is a good speaking voice, combining depth, fullness, and a pleasantness of tone.

A uniformly courteous and gracious manner, a large stock of common sense, a flexible disposition, proper reticence in speech, refinement of taste, and a broad-mindedness expressing itself in nobility and self-sacrifice, are some of the qualities which make for an attractive personality.

They are also important factors in a successful life.

MARCH TWENTY-FIVE

Ideals Are Heights of Inspiration

Set before your mind in clear and definite form one of your great life purposes. Then concentrate upon it for a few minutes each day, in a place where you can be quiet and relaxed.

Direct your mind to it immediately upon rising in the morning, and the last thing upon retiring at night.

Carefully think out the best means and methods for realizing such purpose. Dwell upon the advantages, rewards, and pleasures which will come from its realization.

Confidently believe yourself capable of achieving the great purpose you have in mind.

Be enthusiastic about it. Turn to the contemplation of it at frequent intervals. Resolve to bend your best energies and abilities to its accomplishment.

Ideals are heights of inspiration.

MARCH TWENTY-SIX

Read a Great Book Today

Read principally for enlargement and enrichment of mind. Waste no time on trivial or inferior books. Life should not be squandered on the useless and inconsequential.

Be selective and fastidious in your daily reading. A glorious company of distinguished men of all time invite you to share their best thoughts and sentiments. There is a wealth of noble and inspiring literature at your ready service.

Choose a great book today for your companion. As you read the great thoughts of great men, endeavor so to assimilate their ideas and ideals as to make them a practical power in your life.

Realize the importance of selective and discriminating thought in building a great and worthy life.

As you think, so will your life be.

MARCH TWENTY-SEVEN

Cultivate the Student Habit

Your intellectual power grows through use. You cannot acquire knowledge by proxy. You must store your mind with fundamental truth, and work out your own mental problems.

Develop a habit of clear, logical thinking, of digging deeply to foundation truths and principles. Have a direct, definite, daily plan for mental culture.

Feed your mind upon the thoughts of the world's greatest thinkers. Make good use of spare moments to develop new and useful ideas. Books give you the materials of knowledge, but wisdom must come largely from within yourself. Meditate upon what you read.

Daily reflect upon what you have done, and intend to do. Carefully examine your present methods, and seek to improve them.

Cultivate the student habit.

MARCH TWENTY-EIGHT

Rid Yourself of Personal Faults

There is a host of common faults and habits from which you should persistently endeavor to keep yourself free.

Do not be misled by specious excuses offered on their behalf, but root them out of your nature if they are there.

They are recognized as irritability, intolerance, anger, worry, super sensitiveness, ill-temper, restlessness, sullenness, resentment, moodiness, discourtesy, captiousness, cynicism, impulsiveness, unkindness, false pride, presumption, carelessness, insincerity, indiscretion, selfishness, disloyalty, self-assertion, disparagement, insinuation, and hyper-criticism.

These undesirable characteristics react upon the guilty one, and therefore should be avoided if only for self-interest.

MARCH TWENTY-NINE

Make This Day Great in Results

Ask yourself frankly whether you are conducting your life upon as high a plane as you might, or whether you are satisfied with a standard below your best.

Ask yourself whether you really desire to make the most of your powers and opportunities. If you do so desire, then definitely determine to make this day richer, fuller, and better in aim and achievement than ever before.

Remember that it is by translating your fine sense of aspiration into actual daily deeds that you grow toward your ideal.

Link your lofty thoughts to earnest, active effort, and good results will inevitably follow.

The great things you intend to do some time have a beginning if they are ever to be done, so begin to do something great today.

MARCH THIRTY

Breathe Deeply for Good Health

One of the most important factors in building and maintaining good health is to breathe deeply. Several times daily stop and deliberately take half a dozen or more deep breaths.

Inhale through your nose, and at the same time expand your abdomen and chest to their fullest extent.
Exhale through your mouth, slowly, smoothly, deeply.

Realize that deep breathing cleanses your lungs and fills them with life-giving oxygen. Enjoy the exercise and get the full benefit of its invigorating effect.

Deep breathing is the basis of robust health. Remind yourself many times daily to breathe deeply, and continue this practice until it becomes a subconscious habit.

The last thing at night, take several deep breaths at an open window.

MARCH THIRTY-ONE

The All-Inclusive Goodness of God

The cash-register keeps a man honest, but does not necessarily make him honest.

Abstaining from evil because of the fear of punishment does not destroy evil. The only way to annihilate evil in your life is to realize that it has no power to confer happiness upon you, but on the contrary is a counterfeit and spurious coin masquerading as genuine.

Realize that the only real, enduring, joy-giving power is goodness, and that through right thinking you can be wholly emancipated from belief in sin.

Give some thought daily to eternal truth.

As you spiritualize your mind by understanding the all-inclusive goodness of God, every motive for wrong doing will disappear as mist before the sun, and you will become in actuality a new creature.

APRIL

APRIL ONE

Aim at Consecration and Service

Cultivate dignity, depth, deliberateness, decision and distinction.

Be simple, sincere, serious, serene, sympathetic, and strong. Build courage, confidence, candor, courtesy, concentration, and character. Develop pluck, prudence, perseverance, promptitude, patience, purity, poise, and power.

Consecration of character and purpose should be your constant aim. It is from the mountain heights that you can get the clearest sweep of the horizon.

When you realize that there is a habit which you ought to develop more highly, dwell upon it many times a day. A nail is not driven to its head by a single stroke, nor is a habit formed by a single attempt.

Only repeated effort drives a habit down into the mind so that it becomes deep-rooted and permanent.

APRIL TWO

Growth in Greatness of Character

Much is said of loyalty, love, and service, but their real significance to you is the degree in which you actually use them in your every-day life. Hence you need time for daily meditation and reflection, that you may know what you are doing with your time, talents, and opportunities.

Greatness of character is something more than a catalog of qualities. It is greatness of daily living, intention, conduct, and effort. It is actually doing the things which are implied by greatness. It means an alert mental attitude toward opportunities for noble service.

It is doing promptly and gladly the duty of the moment, without thought of reward or special recognition.

Greatness of life emanates from greatness of thought.

APRIL THREE

Right Talking as a Stimulant

Right talking is a stimulant to right thinking. It serves among other things the great purpose of bringing into view valuable thoughts which otherwise would remain dormant.

It is significant that most of the world's great thinkers met in groups, to exchange ideas and opinions. There is no better way to supplement the results from reading a great book than to talk the subject over with a congenial and well-informed friend.

Thoughts grow and multiply in the process of expression. Uncertain and indefinite thoughts often become clarified when they have been put into actual words.

Talking should always be reciprocal, not exclusive.

To be an interesting talker, you must also be an interesting listener, since one is a complement of the other.

APRIL FOUR

Stepping-Stones to Real Success

You are building better than you realize. Just at the time when things appear to be going the wrong way, they must be shaping themselves for the best results.

A temporary disappointment is often a blessing in disguise. Seeming failure has many a time proved only a stepping-stone to real success.

Every trial, temptation, mistake, and apparent failure can be made to serve a useful purpose. It depends upon yourself whether you turn such experiences to practical advantage. Your best guides and teachers are often those very disappointments which stimulate to better self-management.

Meditate deeply upon a difficult problem, and the solution will probably unfold itself.

There is no such thing as failure to one who makes it a lesson in wisdom.

APRIL FIVE

The Value of Self-Examination

It is easy to offer advice to others, but difficult to apply it to ourselves. There is a natural tendency to tell others what they should and should not do, and to give them profound counsel for the proper conduct of their lives.

Most of us, however, need all the good advice and suggestions we can receive. The time we spend in attempting to influence and direct other people, might often be spent to greater advantage in self-examination, self-improvement, and self-discipline.

We are all in the process of development, and we shall be well advised if we first apply advice to ourselves before offering it to others.

The greatest influence for good in the world is by means of personal example rather than through admonition and exhortation.

APRIL SIX

Render Helpful Service Today

The habit of being uniformly considerate toward others will bring you into increased happiness. As you put into practice the cardinal qualities of patience, punctuality, sincerity, and solicitude, you will have a better opinion of the world around you.

The consciousness of duty well done brings satisfaction and the incentive to do still better.

It is in the little things of every-day intercourse with others that you can best develop sympathetic qualities of heart.

True gentleness is not incompatible with power. It is a mark of nobility of soul.

Be ready to take advantage of trifling opportunities to say the generous word, do the thoughtful act, and render helpful service. You will not pass this way again.

APRIL SEVEN

Cultivate a Yielding Disposition

Adaptability is indispensible to a well-ordered life. It has its basis in unselfishness and discipline, and therefore is quick to adjust itself to difficult and unexpected circumstances.

It is one of the most valuable qualities in times of stress and misunderstanding. It helps to clear the atmosphere of dark clouds of doubt and disagreement.

It enables one to enter sympathetically into the thoughts and feelings of others. It solves many an otherwise stubborn problem.

As you develop in your character the quality of adaptability, you will gradually free yourself from numerous worries, frictions, and embarrassments which beset the average life.

Cultivate a yielding disposition, and interpret generously what others say and do.

APRIL EIGHT

Be Worthy of Your High Calling

The supreme guide to right living is the Word of God as expressed in the Bible. You cannot possibly get away from God.

The great need is for practical righteousness, the truth of God actually applied to every-day life. This priceless truth is to be found in God's Holy Word.

Study it daily, meditate upon it deeply, make it your constant guide and counselor. It will be a lamp to your feet, and a light to your path. It will cultivate with you the fruit of the Spirit: love, joy, peace, long-suffering, gentleness, goodness, faith, meekness, temperance.

Awake, O man, and claim your inestimable inheritance today. Go forth with courage and purpose to your appointed work.

Be worthy of your high calling.

APRIL NINE

Plan Better and Achieve More

Realize how quickly time passes and you will plan better and achieve more. When you have an important thing to do, reserve sufficient time in which to do it properly.

Miscalculation as to time is a prolific cause of haste, waste, inefficiency, inconvenience, and disappointment. It is impossible to do two hours of good work in one.

Know how much you can accomplish in a certain time, then make your plans accordingly. Work that you do hastily or under pressure of time is not likely to be your best work. Plan the hours of the day so that they will yield the best results.

Time passes quickly, and what you do with the present moment is of vital importance.

Definite thought and action economizes time and energy. Beware vacillation.

APRIL TEN

Your Manners, Tastes and Habits

The man you most admire is the type of man you ought to be. He is courteous, adaptable, magnanimous, sympathetic, and tactful. He favors pleasant aspects of life, and has large common sense.

It is well to study this type of man and to emulate his example. The fine qualities of kindliness, tact, sympathy, and courtesy can be cultivated by giving them thoughtful attention.

You can also learn what not to be from the unlovely type of man. He is captious, contradicting, unsympathetic, and phlegmatic. You feel you have nothing in common with him. He repels you. Rather, develop in yourself the manners, tastes, and habits you admire in others.

The man you most like to meet is the type of man you ought to be.

APRIL ELEVEN

Learn to Be Still and Meditate

It is a great gift to be able to sit still and meditate when all around is noise, bustle, and confusion.

The restless spirit in most men is constantly urging them on to some perspiring project, to keep going in the hope of getting at least somewhere, to strain all the energies toward some mighty enterprise.

Application and diligence are desirable qualities to possess, nay essential. However, a well-planned life demands, too, intervals of silence and quietude for mental and spiritual growth, for the building of airy castles, for tracing out detailed plans, and estimating future prospects and possibilities.

The hours you spend in quiet meditation and deliberation are necessary to intelligent planning, living, and working.

APRIL TWELVE

Round Out Your Life into Fullness

The exclusive often excludes itself. Put a barrier between yourself and the world, and you will not so much shut the world from you as you will shut yourself from the world.

Man was not made to live alone. Times of solitude are essential to your greatest growth, but you must also have the society of your fellow men in order to round out your life into fullness.

Exclusiveness is not good when it deprives you of influences and associations which you ought to have.

There is a happy mean between solitude and sociability.

You must have periods with your auto-comrade, when you can hold deep communion with yourself, and appraise your spiritual assets; but it is equally important to mingle with society that you may benefit by its ideas and influence.

APRIL THIRTEEN

Look Earnestly to Your Own Needs

A profound duty devolves upon you to develop daily and assiduously in your own life the qualities of sympathy, sincerity, and sacrifice.

Thus you may contribute your share to the world's improvement and advancement.

The world should grow steadily better, wiser, and nobler, and it will do this in the degree that individual men cultivate these virtues in themselves.

Do not wait for other men to take the first steps in self-improvement, but look earnestly to your own needs and resolve to set a high personal example which other men will see and wish to emulate.

The world grows better because of the men who are consecrated to high thinking and noble deeds.
Your rightful place is with such men.

APRIL FOURTEEN

Be Right, Just, and Magnanimous

Keep your viewpoint broad and generous. Be patient with those whose opinions conflict with yours. No one has the monopoly on truth. You may not be wholly right, and your opponent may not be wholly wrong.

Let your desire be to be right, just, magnanimous, rather than to triumph over the opinions and judgments of other men. Truth eventually justifies itself.

When your motives are right you may stand strong and confident in face of criticism and vituperation.

A sincere and persistent desire for the truth will be your best safeguard against the ignoble and untrustworthy. Tolerance, patience, right motives, and lofty purpose will give you a sense of mental security.

Let your daily life speak eloquently of your ideals.

APRIL FIFTEEN

Use the Best Powers of Your Mind

Love truth for its own sake, not for the reward it will bring to you. Seek good for its own sake, not for the happiness it will confer upon you.

Thus will your life become sweeter and stronger each day, since truth and goodness are the foundation of great and noble living.

Inspired by loftiness or purpose and breadth of mind, you will ascend from one plane of thought to another until your view will be like that from a mountain height.

Petty limitations and false motives will disappear from your mentality, and you will be conscious of having graduated into a vastly larger world of thought and purpose.

The quest for eternal truth is the greatest work to which you can address the best powers of your mind.

APRIL SIXTEEN

Your Privilege and Opportunity

Greatness of manhood implies self-denial and self-sacrifice. Nobility of character demands much service and unselfishness.

As you grow in bigness of spirit, you will more readily yield your personal preferences to the desires of others.

An inward sense of happiness and peace comes from doing voluntarily a noble act, of rendering a secret service which involves self-denial, or of making a special personal sacrifice in the cause of another's welfare.

The spirit of Christ is to give generously, freely, and daily, to render helpful service at every opportunity, to seek deliberately and earnestly to make the world stronger, better, happier, and more beautiful.

This is your rare privilege and opportunity.

APRIL SEVENTEEN

Take an Exalted Place in the World

Desire, definiteness, determination, and daring are necessary to successful achievement in any great endeavor. These supreme qualities have characterized the world's greatest men.

You cannot wish nor dream your way into largeness of life. You must plan and plow and persevere in order to win reward and renown. Life's big prizes and preferences are given to the efficient and worthy.

If you would take an exalted place in the world of workers, you must win your way not by wishing, but through wisdom, will and worthiness. You elect by means of your thought power the precise place you are to occupy.

There is nothing more potent than well-directed thought.

Seize every opportunity to improve yourself.

APRIL EIGHTEEN

Be Yourself at Your Best

You are what you are. No pleasing, pretense, assertion, explanation, or apology can make you other than you are innately.

If you would be other than you are, set to work in the silent and secluded chamber in your own soul, and there begin the work of reformation.

All growth is from within out. A veneering process never changes character. To progress toward perfection, apply yourself persistently and sincerely to mental stocktaking and mental housecleaning.

Put your mind in order, and be fastidious in forming your habits and thoughts. Power in its supreme forms always works noiselessly. Accustom yourself to do everything with regularity, poise, and deliberateness. Be yourself at your best.

You are what you are.

APRIL NINETEEN

As You Think In Your Own Heart

It is literally true that as you sow, so will you reap. It is the immutable and inexorable law, and it applies alike in the physical and mental realms.

The mission of pain is discipline. It acts as a sentinel, a signal, a reformer, warning you of more serious trouble if you do not mend your course.

Your character is the sum of your acts, and each of your acts is preceded by a thought.

Therefore, as you think in your heart, as you daily develop and dwell upon certain thoughts in your own mind, so in reality you are.

Inasmuch as your thoughts are both architect and builder of your life and destiny, you should guard them as your greatest power and possession.

The truth of God is the pearl of great price.

APRIL TWENTY

The Infinite Supply of Good

The supreme spiritual law is that health, harmony, and happiness are directly dependent upon right thinking.

To have right effects in your outward life you must have right causes in your inner mind.

The kingdom of harmony is within you.

It is possible for you to correct every wrong and erroneous condition in your life by the intelligent application of truth.

There is an infinite supply of good for your use, but you must connect yourself with the great source of spiritual law.

There are upward of two billion suns in this galaxy, but what is more wonderful God has graciously bestowed upon you the inestimable gift of making his own thoughts forever available to you.

APRIL TWENTY-ONE

Think and Plan Carefully

At the beginning of each day carefully determine what are the really essential things you should do, then give them first attention. Once you have formed this habit you will have increased sense of satisfaction.

The actual working time of a single day is short, and often many things contemplated and planned for a given day must be postponed.

Take time to think and plan carefully, and you will make each day more highly productive in actual results. Get a right sense of life's values.

Learn to give your thought first to essential things, so that useless trifles will not so easily consume your time.

The more earnestly you study right proportion and perspective, the better judgment you will have in planning a well-ordered life.

APRIL TWENTY-TWO

Silence is Essential to Growth

Silence brings stillness in spirit. Silence promotes clearness and accuracy of mental vision. When you are long silent, you profoundest thoughts tend to disclose themselves.

It is in the silent sanctuary of your own spirit, when you have shut out all worldly thoughts and cares, that you come to intimate communion with the source of all good.

It is then that you become most deeply conscious of your God-given powers. In cultivating a quiet life it must not be allowed to subside into indolence and self-sufficiency.

Times of silence are essential to spiritual growth, but this does not mean detachment and aloofness.

After periods of silence and solitude you should return to society with vastly increased power for sympathy and service.

APRIL TWENTY-THREE

The Practical Use of Meditation

Meditation is a valuable aid in deepening knowledge, correcting judgment, and formulating right plans. By means of meditation you learn to appraise your ideas at their correct value.

When you desire to materialize some important thing in your life, first sit down where you can be silent and undisturbed.

Drop all tension of the mind and body. Then mentally outline the thing you want. Dwell upon it until you can see it clearly and in detail. Study it until it until it becomes as definite as the plans of an architect.

When it is clear and satisfactory to you, concentrate on it until it is deeply impressed upon your mind. Insist upon securing a clear-cut mental picture.

Then proceed day by day to actualize this plan and picture in your life.

APRIL TWENTY-FOUR

Claim Your Freedom and Power

Happiness is a habit. A bright, hopeful, optimistic attitude of mind is essential to your well-being. There is healing power in a single spiritual idea.

Peace, poise, confidence, and contentment are the natural products of a happy disposition. Kindness and appreciation promote happiness. Generosity and good will have an uplifting influence.

To be happy is not only your privilege, but it is your duty. The power which you have to give happiness to others implies an obligation to do so.

Happiness does not depend so much upon great material possessions as upon right mental attitude.

There is nothing which will so surely produce happiness in your own life and that of those about you as a uniform habit of kindness and appreciation.

APRIL TWENTY-FIVE

Seek Earnestly to Know Yourself

The truly great are those who, without sense of humiliation, willingly recognize their own deficiencies and earnestly seek to correct them.

The world does not expect you to know everything, but you can make an earnest effort to know essential things.

You are weak when you are reluctant to acknowledge your ignorance; you are strong when you place the desire to know and understand above mere personal feeling and appearance. Let your desire for truth transcend all minor considerations.

Ignorance is invariably confident. The man of knowledge learns to realize his own needs. Be honest and severe in your self-appraisal. Learn the art of learning, and you are well on the way to achievement.

True greatness is reflective, not assertive.

APRIL TWENTY-SIX

Recognize Things as They Are

Sin is ignorance. Noise is inefficiency. Anger is weakness. Haste is waste. Self-pity is selfishness. Discontent is infirmity. Flattery is foolishness. Pride is littleness. Sloth is extravagance.

Fear is self-limitation. Worry is blindness. Prejudice is narrowness. Envy is meanness. Resentment is obliquity. Arrogance is ill-breeding. Revenge is savagery. Simplicity is greatness. Gentleness is strength. Poise is power.

Righteousness is wisdom. Truth is reality. Faith is aspiration. Generosity is gratitude. Nobility is uprightness. Refinement is sensitiveness. Dignity is high-mindedness.

Patience is discipline. Humility is obedience. Purity is consecration. Holiness is wholeness. Love is unselfishness. Happiness is perfection.

APRIL TWENTY-SEVEN

How to Form Right Habits

Habits that become deeply rooted in your life are often difficult to change. Ordinary resolutions are not usually effective.

Such faults as worry, anger, impulsiveness, resentment, and impatience, can be eliminated only by earnest, persistent, repeated effort.

The first step is to recognize the special defects in your character, and next to take every available means to eradicate them. If you have been thinking the wrong kind of thoughts – thoughts of discouragement, poverty, timidity, limitation – begin at once to substitute the right kind of thoughts – thoughts of encouragement, plenty, confidence, and opportunity.

The process of substituting right thought habits for wrong ones will gradually bring about the desired transformation.

APRIL TWENTY-EIGHT

Practice Quietness and Relaxation

Sit in a quiet place. Relax the entire body. Slowly inhale a full deep breath through the nostrils. Exhale very slowly.

Continue this exercise for a few minutes, breathing slowly, regularly, and deeply.

When you have become quiet and relaxed, direct your mind to such helpful thoughts as peace, contentment, love, truth, goodness, harmony, beauty, kindness, gratitude, health, success, achievement, happiness, independence, and prosperity.

As you continue to apply this exercise at convenient intervals, you will realize that these qualities are becoming more manifest in your life, and that there is no limit to the possibilities of your development along these lofty lines.

Constructive thoughts building your power, progress, and prosperity.

APRIL TWENTY-NINE

Cultivate True Simplicity

Keep your life simple. Be on strict guard against the subtle influences of men and society to lead you away from the simple life.

Keep your life simple in a big, strong sense. True simplicity is free from self-seeking and selfishness. It manifests itself in a sincere and straightforward attitude toward others.

Be true to the visions and inspirations of your own mind. If you would be great you must be simple, sincere, and strong.

The simple things of the world confound the wise.

The last shall be first. Realize the power and greatness of true simplicity, and endeavor to make it a preeminent quality in your character, work, and life.

The noble men of all time have been men of simplicity and sincerity.

APRIL THIRTY

Be a Constant Help to Others

The greatest influence for good that you can wield in the world is by your personal example. You own undeviating devotion to high ideals will do more to encourage and help other men than any verbal counsel you can offer.

The effect of a great example cannot be fully estimated, since it often influences men unconsciously. Probably when you least suspect it you are most influencing those about you. Hence the importance of always being on your best behavior.

Life is a precious thing, and opportunity to do good through example and service imposes a sacred obligation upon each and all.

Let your best self be expressed in your speech, manner, and personality, that you may be a constant help and inspiration to other men.

MAY

MAY ONE

Take Pleasure in Your Work

It is well to work, observe, read, talk, exercise, play, study, and travel, but not to overdo any of these things.

Prudence dictates a happy medium, a middle course, as most conducive to the best results.

Excessive work, continuous observation, protracted talking, and prolonged reading and studying are taxing and tiresome.

To be too much occupied may spell inefficiency. You can be too continually interested, so that your mental and physical powers become sapped and weakened. There is desirable disinterestedness which will prevent you from wasting your energy upon trifles and non-essentials.

Learn to take pleasure in everything you do, whether it be work or play, but always avoid extremes.

Experience should teach prudence and conservatism.

MAY TWO

Think Right and You Will Do Right

You cannot afford to dally with wrong, sinful, undesirable thoughts. It is perilous business to let such thoughts occupy your mind an instant longer than necessary to substitute the right opposite thoughts.

Make a solemn pledge with yourself that you will always destroy such thoughts on the instant of their appearance.

You must not only do right, but your innermost thought and intention should be unwaveringly directed toward the right.

If there is a single unworthy thought slumbering in your mind, root it out today by a thorough mental overhauling. Thoughts are real things, governing, directing and influencing your life and destiny.

Keep your thoughts strong, wholesome, and ascending. Think right and you will do right.

MAY THREE

God's Truth is Now Yours

The voice of truth comes to you most clearly at times of deep meditation. Through spiritual intuition you come into deeper possession of the finer, truer, stronger elements of your God-given self.

As you meditate upon divine ideas, your mind is clarified and your life elevated. God's truth is now and always accessible to you. It offers the most sublime and satisfying study of all time.

The more you meditate upon divine ideas, the more fruitful will your life become. Think what it would mean to you to conform your mind exclusively to spiritual standards.

Realize what it would mean to live up to the vision of what you ought to be.

Your greatest heritage is the privilege of sharing in God's thoughts and of using them as your own.

MAY FOUR

True Humility is Greatness

Obedience and humility are two supreme qualities of a Christian life. Complete submission to divine authority is a difficult thing for most men, but it is essential to right conduct.

True humility is in reality true greatness, although few men seem willing to practice it. Humility is ready to waive its own rights, to accept less than its due, to rate its own claims low.

It is not like diffidence, which distrusts its own powers, nor weakness, which submits passively to insult or humiliation.

True humility is strong yet simple, confident yet modest, intelligently alert yet kind and forgiving.

Christ was the supreme example of these two great qualities: obedient to the Father, and humble toward men.

MAY FIVE

Practice These Exercises Daily

Begin the day, before you rise, with stretching exercises.

1. Lie flat on the back, stretch the left arm overhead six times and return to the side. Repeat with the right arm. Then alternate.

2. With hands clasped, draw the left leg close to the abdomen, bending the knee. Repeat with the right leg, then with both legs.

3. Raise the left leg, keeping the knee straight. Repeat on the right leg, then alternate.

4. Lie on the right side, raise left arm and left leg.

5. Lie on the left side, raise right arm and right leg.

6. Lie face downward. Flex the left leg at the knee, next the right leg, then both legs.

7. Clasp the hands in the small of the back, draw the hands down as far as possible while raising the head. Do each movement six or more times.

MAY SIX

Launch Your Best Ideas Today

The antidote to sorrow, worry, and discouragement is useful occupation. The next best thing to doing a kindly act is to be appreciative of one.

Progress comes from not making the same mistake twice. It is well to be sure that your train of thought is on the right track. Debt and disease are equally destructive.

A thing you don't need is dear at any price. It is far better to live for a man than to die for one.

Do at least one kind act every day, and your life will grow in beauty and power. To hesitate is weakness, to turn back is defeat.

Look for big values in life and you will be more likely to find them. This is the day of days to launch your new ideas and to demonstrate your worth.

The Golden Rule is twelve inches long.

MAY SEVEN

Enrich Your Life By Good Work

It is really quite wonderful how even little daily victories over inertia, weakness, uncertainty, and depression, contribute ultimately to a successful life.

The practice of rising above petty discouragement and seeming obstacles soon develops a habit of self-confidence equal to any undertaking.

Work was never intended to be drudgery, but a source of pleasure and a stimulus to worthy achievement.

Life is not a treadmill, a jail, or a place of punishment, but a beautiful and fascinating field of endeavor and enterprise, with inspiring horizons of newer and greater fields beckoning ever onward.

Work, opportunity, effort, and service are blessings to enrich life and make it truly worth living.

Blessed is the man who does his work joyously.

MAY EIGHT

Give Time Daily to Self-Culture

There are no short cuts to wisdom. The acquisition of superior knowledge demands thoroughness, accuracy, and concentration.

Desultory reading and fitful study may give you information, but not great knowledge and culture.

Ordinary ability with extraordinary diligence can accomplish astonishing results.

Intellectual power is a growth rather than a gift. The inevitable price for real knowledge is laborious application. The use you make of your present mental powers has a vital influence upon your further development.

Intellectual culture is not for self-satisfaction or ostentatious display, but for increased efficiency, usefulness, and achievement.

The time you give daily to self-culture is a profitable investment.

MAY NINE

Accept Your Great Heritage Now

Now is the time for you to assume your rightful place in the world.

Within the realm of your own mind, you have exalted powers which you should put to actual, practical, immediate use.

Your mental power will grow in a marvelous way as you utilize the superior material of your mind.

Realize the great mental resources at your ready command, and resolve to make better and larger use of your daily opportunities. Get a clear mental picture of what you ought to do, then keep it before you as a constant inspiration.

There is an inexhaustible field open for your talents and energies. Do not longer procrastinate, but accept your great heritage now.

All things necessary are yours if you will but take them.

MAY TEN

Take a Strong Stand for Truth

If there is anything in your present habits or character which is preventing you from expressing your real self and living your best life, put it from you now and forever.

Take an uncompromising stand for truth, be done with your timidity and subterfuge, and dare to live with your own convictions.

Once the pathway of right and duty is clear to you, let no influence entice you from it.

Rid yourself once and for all of every weight and obstacle which in the slightest degree retards your highest progress.

Proclaim yourself this day a free man, free to work and serve, free to live the big, sincere, useful, and independent life made possible to you by the gift of God.

Relinquish everything which holds you back from your highest heritage.

MAY ELEVEN

Emulate the Highest Examples

The world always gives its praise to men of sterling principle. You are constantly enjoined to emulate the example of high-minded men who put character above covetousness and righteousness above mere personal power.

Many of the greatest men have performed common and ordinary duties with the same thoroughness and spirit demanded by great tasks.

The seemingly commonplace duties of daily life have an important part in developing the industry, perseverance, and courage essential in large affairs.

To become a leader and an authority in any field of activity, you must first apprentice yourself to the daily round and routine of seemingly insignificant things.

Make the best of what you have, and greater things will follow.

MAY TWELVE

Think Well Before You Speak

Ill-considered speech is responsible for many misunderstandings and enmities.

There is nothing so inimical to friendship as the habit of impulsive and imprudent speaking.

There are indiscreet talkers who never take time to estimate the possible damage of what they say, but turn blithely from one subject to another seemingly unconscious of having given personal offense.

There is no more dangerous weapon than an unruly tongue, and it has well been called the great divider.

Set, therefore, a seal on your lips, put a bridle on your tongue, and think well before you speak.

It is your duty to speak, but it is will always to remember that you proclaim yourself to the world through silence as well as through speech.

MAY THIRTEEN

Put Forth Your Best Efforts

There is inspiration in the thought that genius thrives upon the impossible. To the man of confidence and courage, difficulties serve only to stimulate and enlist the highest efforts of which he is capable.

No one knows the real difficulties, discouragement, and demands of a work until he is engaged in it.

No matter how formidable a task may appear to you, if it is a work to which you believe yourself called, put forth your best abilities, and difficulty will readily surrender to diligence.

The man of great capacity naturally seeks a great enterprise. Your physical and mental powers grow best in the exercise of adequately laborious tasks.

One of the greatest rewards of achievement is that it lights the way to something still greater.

MAY FOURTEEN

Good Is Always Available to You

Rebuke in yourself every weakness and shortcoming. Be diligent in your desire for the best in daily life.

Daily commit to memory some great thought that it may quicken and ennoble you. Be ready and willing to part with your faults. Have the courage to be simple and sincere in all your thoughts and acts.

The only thing higher than the wish to serve is to render service. It is in the common incidents of your daily life that you reveal your true character.

Good is always available to you. This inexhaustible power is at your command at any moment and in every emergency.

Claim your great heritage today. The best is forever yours, and God cooperates with you if you but diligently seek Him.

You are of God, and so should you walk.

MAY FIFTEEN

Ideals Are Valuable as Incentives

One of the most important things in the building of personal character is to correct in yourself every fault as promptly as you discover it.

Willingly to acknowledge your faults is a first step to eliminating them. Persistent faults and weaknesses must be persistently combated and corrected.

Look at your faults fearlessly and critically. Do not let your weak qualities dominate your life.

Your best self is represented by your best qualities.

Live therefore according to the best that is in you, and make every day contribute something substantial to your highest development.

Ideals are valuable as incentives, but their real and enduring worth is the measure in which they lead you to actual achievement.

MAY SIXTEEN

Work on Clear and Definite Lines

Avoid the common habit of undertaking too many things at a time. Do one thing well and you will be better prepared to undertake the next thing. By this method you will avoid confusion and anxiety.

Take time to do what is best and most important for you to do. Be particularly vigilant against squandering time on trifles.

The more you work along clear and definite lines the more you will accomplish. Attempting only one thing at a time and doing it thoroughly will bring a satisfying sense of progress.

Make it your special object to finish at least one definite worth-while thing each day. Clearly outline a single purpose in your mind and be quite sure to achieve it.

It is surprising how such daily undertakings will multiply into something great and gratifying.

MAY SEVENTEEN

Use the Power of Self-Suggestion

Just as you are unconsciously influenced by outside advertisement, announcement, and appeal, so can you vitally influence your life from within by auto-suggestion.

The first thing each morning, and the last thing at night, suggest to yourself specific ideas which you wish to embody in your character and personality.

Address such suggestions to yourself, silently or aloud, until they are deeply impressed upon your mind.

Repeat them many times, and continue the exercises daily until you are satisfied that the desired ideas are being materialized.

As you use the power of self-suggestion, you will realize more fully its wonderful influence in developing purpose, diligence, accuracy, definiteness, and other valuable personal qualities.

MAY EIGHTEEN

Your Life Is Built on Faith

It is generally recognized that faith is a great vital force in the conduct of human affairs. It plans an essential part in business, education, medicine, politics, science and religion.

Faith is the master-key to great discovery, invention and achievement.

Faith is not blindness, supposition, credulity, or ordinary belief. Belief is of the intellect, faith is of the soul. Faith overleaps all visible horizons.

Daily you will act and walk by faith rather than by sight. You are constantly exercising faith whether you are conscious of it or not. Your life is built on faith.

The antidote for worry, fear, anxiety, doubt, discontent, and other disturbing elements is a supreme faith in God, in men, and in your-self.

MAY NINETEEN

Think About the Things You Want

Stop thinking of the things you don't want, and think more about the things you do want.

Stop thinking and talking about war, armaments, dreadnoughts, disaster, poverty, hard times, bad luck, panic, crime, evil, failure, suicide, discord, disease, and death.

Think and talk more about peace, plenty, health, life, opportunity, confidence, happiness, progress, power, prosperity, achievement, truth, success, justice, and righteousness.

Your thoughts help to make the world what it is. Try to make the world what it should be. Substitute cooperation for competition, love for hate, trust for suspicion, peace for war, and service for selfishness.

Right thinking is the greatest power in the world to establish peace and good-will among men.

MAY TWENTY

Put Your Plan into Execution

Before you retire at night, make a mental plan of the important things you intent to do the next day.

When you have a well-made plan, and earnestly resolve to fulfill it, you will accomplish more in less time and with less expenditure of energy than you would do otherwise.

The essential thing is to carry out your plan conscientiously. Assuming that you have made it as a result of intelligent consideration, adhere to it strictly.

Put purpose, resoluteness, and faith into your work, that every day may be highly productive.

Great achievement is the sum of many small acts.

Devote your superior abilities to significant things, so that you may ultimately realize a great life purpose.

Aspiration must precede achievement.

MAY TWENTY-ONE

Become Master of Your Moods

You are frequently subjected to mental tests, when you must choose what course to take. A mood of depression creeps over you, or a sense of disappointment would make you captive. Submit to it, and it will possibly master you.

Reason it out quietly and logically, and you can deprive it of its power to enslave you. Just as wrong thinking has brought depression and disappointment to you, so right thinking can emancipate you from its influence.

Take ample time for meditation, that your thoughts may deepen and mature.

Realize that you serve your best ultimate interests by promptly ridding your mind of every discordant thought, and that persistent effort of the right kind will surely make you master of your moods and circumstances.

MAY TWENTY-TWO

Realize the Joy of Hard Work

The worst thing that can befall you is to have nothing useful to do. From that moment life will be an aimless, aching void, and time a cruel torturer.

The man who has not experienced the joy of hard work has lived in vain. A life of ease and sloth is a daily purgatory and a cause of widespread unhappiness.

It is incomprehensible that in this day of golden opportunity there should be anyone, in good health, with nothing to work and live for.

The joy of work, of daily conquest, of unexpected difficulties to overcome, of new enterprises – these make life interesting, worthwhile, and wholesome.

Find your right vocation, put your abilities to daily use, work cheerfully, willingly, and courageously, and you will know the joy of true living.

MAY TWENTY-THREE

Make Definite Daily Progress

Indecision and inaction are foes to progress. When you are in doubt about an important course of conduct take time to consider it thoroughly.

Cultivate a judicial mind and weigh all sides of the matter. Form your conclusions slowly and deliberately.

Be prudent in your decisions. It is well to think and plan before you act, but once the way is clear to you, go forward with promptitude, resolution, and confidence.

Definite daily steps in the right direction will bring you at length to the desired destination. A progressive life demands initiative, effort and purpose. The law is use or lose.

Today's opportunities will probably never come to you again. Other opportunities may come, but what they will be only time to disclose.

MAY TWENTY-FOUR

Conform Your Life to God's Plan

Be sincere in your self-judgment. If there is any moral imperfection, false pride, indolence, or indulgence, look at it fearlessly and resolve to conform your life to God's perfect plan.

Do not defraud yourself by passing lightly over faults which you know should be eradicated from your nature.

Subject yourself to a rigid self-examination, and having found the weak and imperfect things proceed to substitute and develop the qualities which distinguish greatness of character.

Know precisely what you are now and what you intend to be. Know your true motives.

Remember there is nothing finer than a spirit of sincere service, which gives generously without thought of recognition or return.

True greatness lies in giving rather than in receiving.

MAY TWENTY-FIVE

Spiritualize Your Thought Habits

The significance of your good thoughts may not now be wholly apparent to you, but as such thoughts are multiplied day by day there will come to you a realization of their value in producing greatness of character.

Every good thought you think contributes its share to the ultimate result of your life.

Constantly guard your mind, therefore, against destructive ideas, and store it with helpful, progressive, constructive thoughts. The good thought you think is its own reward, since every such thought has an uplifting influence upon life.

Obviously the only remedy for wrong thoughts is the substitution of right thoughts.

As your thought becomes spiritualized, you will wish to give more love, loyalty, and service to God.

MAY TWENTY-SIX

Cultivate Constructive Thought

In your consciousness you conduct the great commerce of daily thought.

Every thought you think and cultivate contributes something to the sum total of your life mind has a certain capacity for thought.

To clear your mind of erroneous, useless, destructive thoughts, substitute and diligently cultivate right thoughts.

Take one wrong thought at a time and patiently substitute for it the opposite right thought. The divine counsel is to overcome evil with good.

This is the supreme command. If the offense comes in the form of injustice, envy, suspicion, selfishness, dishonesty, or revenge, instantly apply the remedy of thinking only good, and seeming miracles will take place. You can demonstrate this truth for yourself.

MAY TWENTY-SEVEN

Your Mind Grows Through Use

Thought is the greatest power in the world, therefore be a serious thinker. Daily train yourself to think clearly, deeply, accurately.

Be a student of serious subjects. Set apart a few minutes daily for profound and concentrated meditation.

Do not take important things for granted, but examine causes and effects for yourself.

Your mind grows through use. Select and important problem, and study it carefully until you have found a satisfactory solution. You should have an hour for special mental gymnastics every day, bringing all your faculties into full play and activity.

Thought is supreme in all successful business, invention, enterprise, and achievement.

Thought is the greatest power in the world.

MAY TWENTY-EIGHT

Make Sure and Definite Progress

Put into actual practice now the splendid things you confidently expect to do at some future time, and your life will be wonderfully transformed.

Thousands of people have made the serious mistake of thinking that at a more favorable time, or under other circumstances, they would radically change their habits, plans, methods, aims, and ideals.

The only real assurance of your sincere desire to elevate your life is your willingness to initiate some of the desired changes now.

This is the only intelligent course for you if you are to make sure and definite progress. Many a deferred resolution ends in nothing.

What you think you will do some other time may never come to pass, but what you accomplish today is a substantial certainty.

MAY TWENTY-NINE

Advance to Honorable Position

Put forever out of your mind all anxious and self-limiting thoughts. Bend your best efforts toward the big and essential things of life.

Intelligent aspiration, coupled with diligent work, will steadily advance you to high and honorable position. There are wonderful powers and possibilities with you waiting to be utilized.

Make definite choice today of the material you intend to use from this great inner storehouse.

Draw generously, since you cannot possibly exhaust the supply. When you realize fully the immense and inexhaustible mental resources at your command, you will not look to other men for assistance.

Your personal powers are sufficient to give you a distinguished place in the world.

MAY THIRTY

Use Words With Discrimination

Beware the squandering of words. Have times of silence and times of speech. Avoid extremes. It is better to be silent much than to talk much.

Talkativeness is depleting to both talker and listener. When you are inclined to verbosity, put a seal upon your lips and take mental stock of yourself. The words you use proclaim you to the world. They disclose unmistakably your taste, temperament, education, ideals, and degree of culture.

Choose words with the same discrimination that you choose friends. Realize the significance and power of words as living things.

Study words daily and always use them worthily. Correct a fault in your speech the instant you detect it.

Eternal vigilance is the price of great accomplishment.

MAY THIRTY-ONE

Make Every Day Count for Progress

Do not let trifles disturb your tranquility of mind. The little pin-pricks of daily life, when dwelt upon and magnified, may do great damage, but if ignored or dismissed from thought, will disappear from inanition.

Most men have worried about things which never happened, and more men have been killed by worry than by hard work.

Life is so great in its opportunities and possibilities, that you should rise confidently above the inevitable trifles incident to daily contact with the world.

Life is too precious to be sacrificed for the non-essential and transient.

Stand up to the supremacy of your manhood, claim your birthright, dare to go forward, ignore the inconsequential, make every day count for progress, and so will you prosper.

JUNE

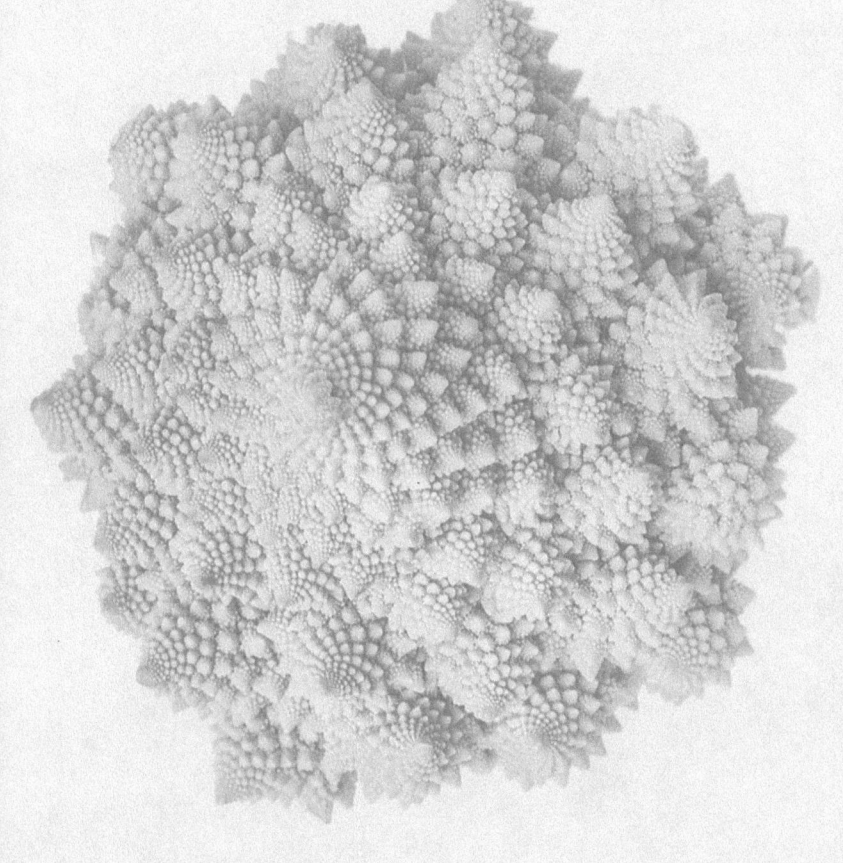

JUNE ONE

Analyze Your Motives and Habits

Make a practical plan for your spiritual culture. Put it in writing, and once you have decided it is the best plan you can make, adhere strictly to it.

Carefully analyze your motives and impulses, to determine which should be encouraged and which restrained. A definite plan will enable you to resist undesirable tendencies and to pursue intelligently the essentials of spiritual development.

The highest purpose of your life is to grow in spiritual grace, strength, and symmetry. There are noble powers within you which give assurance of immensely larger things than you have yet realized.

Goodness, righteousness, and truth are fruits of the Spirit, and as you cultivate these supreme qualities you will grow in likeness to God.

JUNE TWO

Reason Out Things for Yourself

Cultivate beliefs. Through earnest study and investigation translate your opinions into convictions.

Look deeply into important subjects. Be thorough in your mental habits. Accustom yourself to trace out successive steps from cause to conclusion.

Be sure to have adequate reasons for your beliefs. Broadly see all sides of a subject. Search out truth for its own value, not for display.

Realize the importance of having settled convictions about the great subjects of life. Take the necessary time to reason out things for yourself, and to secure clear, definite, well-supported ideas.

Make a written list of your leading opinions, beliefs, and convictions. Study them closely, and correct everything doubtful and erroneous.

JUNE THREE

Your Direct Alliance with God

Divine mind is omnipresent. The Mind of God fills all space and is therefore always available.

When you think a good thought, you reflect the Infinite Mind from which all good emanates. Spiritual things are spiritually discerned.

True wisdom comes from meditation upon spiritual ideas. Justice, truth, mercy, love, goodness, and purity, are fruits of the spirit.

The solution off your personal problems is to seek first the Infinite Mind for ideas of truth and righteousness and to use them in your daily life.

Divine mind is always ready to cooperate with you, and to assist you in every right undertaking.

Once assured of this direct alliance with God you will tend to do everything with relation to Him.

JUNE FOUR

Exercise Your Own Facilities

In order to develop great intellectual power you must exercise your own faculties. Knowledge which you acquire through your own diligence and application will become your most useful and permanent possession.

When you pay the price of personal labor and perseverance for your knowledge, you will more fully appreciate its value.

Teachers can do much, but there cannot be great intellectual culture without indefatigable work on the part of the student.

Self-imposed tasks of difficulty are an effective means to mental growth and culture. Your most substantial mental progress will depend principally upon your personal efforts.

Continue the student habit throughout your life.
An earnest mind is always learning.

JUNE FIVE

Cultivate Desirable Qualities

Don't contradict, argue, interrupt, grumble, gossip, antagonize, boast, offend, contend, insinuate, retaliate, depreciate, irritate, intimidate, exaggerate, equivocate, calumniate, resent, retort, reproach, ridicule, resist, coerce, disparage, dissemble, wrangle, malign, misjudge, harangue, slander, embarrass, vilify, assail, nor misrepresent.

Learn to praise, enjoy, affirm, approve, appreciate, serve, reverence, commend, agree, admire, please, encourage, sympathize, yield, reciprocate, accede, forgive, help, recommend, esteem, give, honor, stimulate, acquiesce, respect, protect, befriend, gladden, uphold, accommodate, cheer, console, uplift, compliment, benefit, strengthen, comfort, inspirit, and inspire.

JUNE SIX

Plan Better and Achieve More

Deliberateness does not mean dallying, not squandering time. To do things deliberately is to proceed with regularity, poise, and system.

There are daily routine matters which should be disposed of briskly, but not in nervous haste.

The habit of deliberateness can be combined advantageously with energy and promptitude.

As you realize the fleeting character of time, and the small number of actual working hours in the day, you will plan better and accomplish more. Impulse and haste are responsible for many mistakes and disappointments.

Deliberateness confers the advantages of self-mastership.

There are times when you should increase your ordinary pace, but even then be sure to keep your serenity and self-possession.

JUNE SEVEN

Your Opportunities and Privileges

Waste no time over vain regrets, losses, nor disappointments. Be grateful for present opportunities and privileges.

Bend your mind and energies to the work that now lies before you.

The remedy for worry, anxiety, and fear is to have new interests and responsibilities. Today offers you ample pursuits, pleasures, and problems to engage your best powers.

Take all reasonable measures to avoid repetition of past mistakes, plan intelligently, and be hopeful of the best results.

Be a sensible optimist, realize your immense resources, carry yourself confidently, work industriously, and be assured all will be well with you.

Keep your mind open to truth. Right thinking always yields a harvest of right results.

JUNE EIGHT

Have a Mental Housecleaning

At the close of each day, critically examine your thoughts and acts and note wherein you have done well or otherwise. Daily self-examination will enable you to remedy any defects in your personality. The ledger of your life is a more important matter than your bank-book.

What you have deeded to the credit of your character at the end of the day is of vastly greater value than the number of dollars you have accumulated.

What you have carried to the credit of your soul at the end of your earthly life will count for more than accumulated lands and money.

Have a mental housecleaning every little while. Look into the corners of your mind and clear out accumulated mental rubbish.

Be vigilant and thorough in eliminating every useless thought.

JUNE NINE

Closely Scrutinize Your Beliefs

Your beliefs largely govern you, whether they are true or not. An erroneous belief may lead you into most disastrous results.

The more tenaciously you hold to false beliefs the more injurious will be their destructive influence in your life.

Many intelligent men frankly acknowledge that they do not want the false and untrue, but are unwilling to make the effort to understand and apply the truth.

Closely scrutinize your beliefs, and be eager to strengthen them where they are weak and to change them where they are wrong.

Truth is the only basis upon which to found beliefs that will serve you in all the varied experiences in life.

Truth is the solid rock upon which to build a life of happiness.

JUNE TEN

Take God Into Close Partnership

When a man has a clear and vital realization of his eternal alliance with God, his daily life will be filled with uplifted thought, earnest work, and high ideals. He will carry with him an indescribable sense of confidence and happiness, and an unwavering faith equal to every opportunity, emergency, and obligation.

The privilege of knowing God, of sharing in his love and truth, of communing with him anywhere at any time, belongs to every man.

Hence it is that every man chooses for himself whether or not he will take God into intimate partnership in his daily thoughts and affairs.

Thousands of Christian men have demonstrated the practical value of a close alliance with God, and of looking solely to him for guidance and wisdom.

JUNE ELEVEN

Silence Gives Rest and Power

Great is the power of silence. There is nothing more eloquent than the still, small voice of conscience.

Think of the silent growth of the giant forest. The world upon which you now stand is whirling silently through space. The greatest forces of nature are silent.

How wonderful is the silent power of truth, constantly at work, without effort, sound, or confusion.

Only man is wasteful, prodigally squandering words, speech, and effort. Silence will help you to solve the most difficult personal problems.

Silence is golden. Silence will give you rest from inordinate ambition and desire. Silence promotes quietness of spirit.

The more you cultivate a spirit of inward silence, the better you will have intercourse with God.

JUNE TWELVE

The Importance of Drinking Water

Drink copiously of pure water. Drink six or more glasses of water daily between meals. Do not neglect this important habit.

Drink a glass of water the first thing on rising and the last thing on retiring. Pure water cleanses and renews the system. It is one of the best and most available means for keeping the body pure and healthy.

Always drink slowly. Appreciate the value of pure water, and enjoy it as you drink it. In ill-health drink distilled water.

Avoid extremely hot or cold drinks. At home, in the office, or elsewhere, arrange to have a proper supply of pure drinking water as an indispensible aid to good health.

Once you have formed this habit you will appreciate its practical value and importance.

JUNE THIRTEEN

As You Think, So You Build

Make an inventory of your mental assets. Take stock of yourself and know precisely what you are doing with your thought, time, talents, and energy. Put your mind in order.

Thought rules the world. Everything that is wrought out in the material form is first constructed in the mind. As you think, so you build. Store your mind daily with great thoughts of great thinkers. Frequent contact with master minds will elevate your taste and enlarge your intellectual outlook.

Realize your responsibility to maintain a constantly high standard of thought. Thoroughly discipline your desires, habits, and efforts.

Give some time regularly to mental and moral culture, that you may grow in aspiration and achievement.

There is nothing really commonplace to a lofty intellect.

JUNE FOURTEEN

The Quickening Power of Wisdom

A great statesman attributed his uniform serenity of mind to this motto hung at the foot of his bed where he could read it every day: "Thou wilt keep him in perfect peace whose mind is stayed on thee: because he trusteth in thee."

The quickening power of a wise saying, or a great promise, is inestimable. There are thousands of beautiful mottoes which inspire a drooping spirit with new faith and courage.

All that is sometimes needed to bridge a difficulty, or solve a serious problem, is a little more self-reliance.

The study of great sayings enriches the mind, develops the character, and gives a sense of self-confidence so necessary to successful work.

Literature is filled with wisdom for your personal betterment.

JUNE FIFTEEN

The Significance of Your Life

The highest conception of God is that He is a Being of infinite life, love, goodness, wisdom, and power.

The highest conception of man is that he is made in the image of God, and reflects, in degree, the qualities of his Maker.

As you more fully realize this exalted alliance, you will feel a sense of increased power and responsibility. You will more earnestly seek to do better and bigger things with your God-given abilities. You will have a clearer sense of the significance of possibilities of your life. You will wish to prove worthy of your high calling. You will become obedient to the divine will.

God being all-intelligent knows all about you, knows how to guide, counsel, guard, and protect you.

Keep close to God.

JUNE SIXTEEN

Direct Your Energy Wisely

Few persons can afford to indulge in worry, since it is an extravagant habit. It costs much, while it produces nothing by way of useful results.

Nine-tenths of the things worried about never happen.

Worries are principally of two kinds: of things you cannot help, or of things you can help. If you cannot help them, worry is obviously unavailing and useless. If you can help them, intelligence would indicate that you can take definite steps to remedy them.

In most cases, if the thought and time spent in anxiety and regret were directed to earnest effort in improving present conditions, the useless worry would disappear of itself.

Worry is not a necessary evil, but valuable energy misdirected.

Cultivate contentment through occupation.

JUNE SEVENTEEN

Prove Your Greatness of Character

You have never before had so many opportunities and incentives summoning you to large effort.

What you do with your present chances, abilities, and inspirations, you will be likely to do with larger powers in time to come.

Prove the greatness of the qualities within you by earnest and enthusiastic effort this day. Procrastination is not only the thief of time, but of ambition, initiative, and courage.

Do not mislead yourself into believing that under other circumstances, or in a different environment, you could and would do better. In your present position you can prove your greatness of character.

Right where you are at this moment is the place to begin your best work and to translate your good intentions into actual deeds.

JUNE EIGHTEEN

Build Supreme Personal Qualities

Make a list of the personal qualities which you know have been characteristic of eminently successful men.

You will likely set down such as these: Industry, concentration, self-reliance, integrity, patience, cheerfulness, common sense, energy, self-confidence, tact, enthusiasm, determination, diligence, decision, definiteness, pluck, tenacity, and stability.

When you have made a complete list, submit yourself to a rigid examination to determine approximately in what degree you have already developed these qualities within yourself.

This is a practical plan for uncovering possible weaknesses, and of knowing where to concentrate your efforts toward self-improvement. You can turn this suggestion to your immediate advantage.

JUNE NINETEEN

Faith Gives Assurance of Success

Build your faith sufficiently and there is no reasonable achievement beyond your powers. Faith is a vital part of every great enterprise.

Faith is the master key which unlocks the doors of opportunity. Faith is the power which enables you to undertake every duty with confidence in the final results.

Faith always tends to mental and physical health. Faith illumines the pathway and dissipates shadows and suspicions.

Faith encourages you to persevere in face of doubt and difficulty. Faith gives assurance of success tho the day looks dark and dreary.

Give more of your time to the study and development of faith, and your whole life will become vitalized, broadened, and elevated.

JUNE TWENTY

Suggestions for Building Health

Physical exercises, intended to build vitality and endurance, should be slow, smooth, regular, and rhythmical. Special apparatus is not necessary and often undesirable.

The best exercises are done with the arms and legs, combining stretching, relaxing, and tensing movements.

Violent exercise may lead to muscle stiffness, and should be avoided. The tired business or professional man sometimes needed change and relaxation rather than strenuous physical exercise.

Extreme fatigue is detrimental to robust health. The man of fifty many need a gentler form of exercise than the man of thirty.

Moderation should be the rule here as in other things.

Fresh air is an indispensable ally of good health.

JUNE TWENTY-ONE

Summer is the Time of Gladness

It is the glad of summertime! Days of flowers, sunshine, and blue skies. Days of beauty, freedom, and joyousness. Days of perfume, sweetness, and music.

Mountains, skies, seas, forests, and valleys in all their ineffable charm and harmony. Nature in full and perfect bloom, showering her gifts with lavish prodigality.

Fragrant blooms, crystal streams, dancing shadows, wooing winds, warbling birds, lowing herds, and everywhere the note of unaffected contentment and happiness.

It is the world's holiday time. It is the most beautiful of all seasons, with its foliage and flowers, brightening fields, wistful skies, and dreamy and magical lights.

Summer is the singing, dancing, joy-making time of the human heart.

JUNE TWENTY-TWO

Make a Good Beginning Today

Life is fleeting. Now is the time to initiate your new plan. Today is the day to attempt the great and worthy purpose which you have long had in contemplation.

Delays are dangerous. Procrastination weakens purpose. Seize your opportunity while it is within your reach.

Put forth your most earnest effort, and good results will surely follow. The instant you attempt something fine and great you are on your way to its realization.

All great achievement is a series of progressive steps. All great men have first put forth small efforts, which have led to large works and results.

Let this encourage you to make a vigorous beginning today, so that your dreams and aspirations may become actualized in your life.

JUNE TWENTY-THREE

Think Good Thoughts All the Time

Systematically cultivate the habit of right thinking. Substitute good thought for evil thought and the latter will gradually be eliminated.

Do not parley nor compromise with any kind of wrong thought. The only way to get rid of it effectually is through the power of right thinking.

If it is a desirable thing to think good thoughts part of the time, it is a desirable thing to think good thoughts all of the time, and it is just as easy to think right thoughts as it is the think wrong thoughts.

The habit of right thinking will confer upon you inestimable advantages and blessings. When you think right and do right, your daily life will assume a new and larger significance.

True independence and self-confidence are based upon right thinking.

JUNE TWENTY-FOUR

The Right Use of Conversation

It is a good rule never to flatly contradict another. There are polite ways of dissenting. You may use such ingratiating phrases as, "Have you thought of this view of the matter?" "What do you think of so-and-so's opinion?" "Someone has suggested this idea," or "It might be well to consider this aspect of the question."

Conversation should not antagonize by contradiction or the use of injudicious expressions.

Guard yourself assiduously against everything in word or manner which might cause friction between you and the listener.

Observe the methods of popular speakers and profit by their example.

Conversation should not be used for enforcing personal opinions, but for the courteous interchange of pleasant and helpful ideas.

JUNE TWENTY-FIVE

Cultivate Your Mental Garden

To cultivate a beautiful garden you must uproot all weeds and other unlovely things. This is best done not by sitting down and studying the origin of such weeds, and ascertaining their names and number, but by patience and diligent work in pulling them up by the roots and ridding your garden of them forever.

Likewise to cultivate a beautiful mind you must uproot and cast from you all mental weeds and other unlovely thoughts, such as pride, envy, impatience, fear, resentment, and selfishness.

Then you must plant and carefully cultivate in your mental garden seeds of kindness, goodness, love, purity, humility, reverence, and righteousness.

As you persevere in the work, your mind will gradually unfold into beauty and fragrance, and you life will be blessed.

JUNE TWENTY-SIX

Keep a Clear Purpose Before You

Be grateful for the opportunity to work and serve. Keep a definite purpose before you, and bend it accomplishment your best abilities.

Put the strength of your mind and personality into the urgent duty of the hour, that it may be well and thoroughly done.

Good work is a divine provision for developing in you initiative, self-reliance, diligence, and other sterling qualities.

Do what you have to do in a true spirit of gladness and gratitude, make the fresh beginning of this day an occasion for stronger and better resolutions, and let the close of the day witness to your new acquisitions, graces, and accomplishments.

Today belongs to you, with its inestimable opportunities for work, achievement, and human helpfulness.

JUNE TWENTY-SEVEN

How to Rid Yourself of Worry

When you feel a mood of worry or depression stealing over you, take a quick bath, stretch yourself out flat on the bed, and relax the entire body.

Take deep abdominal breaths, raise first one arm, then the other, letting them drop limply at the sides.

Repeat the exercise with each leg. After you have thoroughly relaxed your body, call to mind a happy incident of your life and dwell upon it.

Soon you will realize that your worry has disappeared. As you continue to substitute uplifting and constructive thoughts, your depression will gradually dissolve into nothingness where it belongs.

The best time to annihilate worry is when it first appears.

Do not parley with it. Strike quickly and the victory is yours.

JUNE TWENTY-EIGHT

Maintain a Right Mental Attitude

Form the habit of standing and sitting erect at all times. Frequently remind yourself to straighten your spine.

Resist the common tendency to lounge. When you are erect the organs of your body more freely and naturally perform their functions. Moreover, an upright carriage is an indication of self-respect and personal dignity.

Make the most of yourself. Carry your head level, your shoulders well back, chest high, and always breathe deeply.

Maintain a right mental attitude, so that it will reflect itself in the way you stand, sit, and walk.

Remember, too, that hopeful thoughts and high ideals have a direct and uplifting effect upon your body, and that to travel optimistically is to speed your footsteps.

JUNE TWENTY-NINE

Cultivate a Yielding Disposition

There is no more valuable lesson for you to learn than that of patiently bearing opposition.

When you express an opinion, welcome contrary ideas as a means of confirming your opinion if it is valid and of correcting it if it is wrong.

Self-opinionated people often close their minds to wisdom and lose valuable opportunities for advancement toward truth. It is well to weigh both sides of a subject before you reach a final decision.

Cultivate a yielding disposition. The truth cannot be monopolized. If you are right you can afford to be patient with one who is wrong.

If you are sincerely seeking the truth, you will always give a ready and patient ear to the views of others.

Truth never fears opposition.

JUNE THIRTY

Essential Steps to Knowledge

The principal object of your reading should be for the acquisition of useful knowledge, and the strengthening, refining, and ennobling, of your character.

Discriminate in your choice between good books and the best books. It is an excellent plan to have a great book always at your ready hand for convenient reading.

Thus you can turn to good account many odd moments which otherwise would be squandered. It is surprising how even a little daily reading, continued for a few weeks or months, will multiply into something highly productive.

The great books of the world's master minds are at your service, to use for your mental and spiritual culture.

Three essential steps to knowledge are realization, assimilation, and utilization.

JULY

JULY ONE

God's Infinite Supply of Thoughts

Flowers are symbols of God's thoughts. The symmetry and sweetness of the tiniest flower are an expression of God's miraculous power.

When you dwell upon a beautiful blossom you are listening to the voice of God who speaks to you through the multiform manifestations of flower and foliage.

God's expression is always eloquent, harmonious, and perfect. It is your inestimable privilege to draw upon His infinite supply of thoughts and to use them as your own.

As you look upon bud and blossom, tree and mountain, sky and sea, listen to the voice of God that you may hear the divine messages which they convey.

The beauty and power of nature all about you tell a wonderous story of God's love and wisdom.

JULY TWO

Culture is of the Mind and Heart

The sovereign remedy for every discordant and undesirable condition in your life is within yourself.

The primary cause of depression, worry, anxiety, sin, failure, fear, and doubt is mental. Determine resolutely to rid yourself of the enemies lurking in the recesses of your own mind.

Take stock of your mental assets, motives and habits. Correct or eliminate everything in your inner life which retards your best progress.

Keep a high ideal constantly before you to stimulate your best powers into activity. Character and culture are inseparable.

Greatness cannot be successfully counterfeited. The sources of nobility are within.

Your character is the product of your daily thought and aspiration. Culture is of the mind and heart.

JULY THREE

Charm and Nobility of Character

Charm is an innate quality of mind and heart, and an expression of a beautiful attitude toward life. Courtesy can be cultivated, but charm is largely an unconscious possession.

Manners are often an exterior polish, assumed for occasion and circumstance, but charm is intrinsic and spontaneous.

Charm is akin to culture, and it is impossible to have either one in high degree without the other. While charm is innate, it can in degree be cultivated.

But to do so it is necessary to go directly to inner sources, to give special attention to the development of the graces of kindness, sincerity, integrity and nobility.

Charm almost baffles definition, yet it is quickly recognized by the world.

JULY FOUR

Live Now Your Highest Life

Deliberately develop in yourself the supreme habits which make for true greatness of life. Many a habit forms involuntarily, and plays its part in determining the degree of your success.

Be on your guard, therefore, in the important matter of habit-making, and be quite sure that you are using each day's opportunities to the best advantage.

Habit has been well described as a cable, weaving only a thread at a time, but at last so strong that it cannot easily be broken.

Eliminate in yourself every weak and undesirable habit. Take a determined stand for everything which enlarges and ennobles your mind.

Resolve to live your highest possible life where you are today. Take stock of your habits.

Character comes from repeated choice.

JULY FIVE

Let Divine Truth Guide You

Your life is the product of repeated thoughts. A good life is a record of good thoughts.

The more you multiply good thoughts the better your life will be. Good thoughts produce health and happiness.

As all good comes from God, you must go to God from your supply of good. The habit of daily reading the Bible will store your mind with rich treasures of divine wisdom. Proverbs, the Psalms, and the Gospels, will give you truth, instruction, and inspiration.

Let divine truth guide you in all your thoughts, plans, and ideals.

God is the infinite source of supply, and He pours forth His riches to you in abundant measure, and they are yours to take if you will.

He that soweth to the Spirit shall of the Spirit reap life everlasting.

JULY SIX

Conserve Your Personal Powers

It is the petty pin-pricks of daily life which do the most mischief. Doing avoidable and unnecessary things squanders mental and physical vitality.

The energy and earnestness you apply to large tasks does not deplete your force. The strain comes from nervousness, anger, irritability, haste, worry, and excitement. Be on your guard against leakages of nerve force.

Resolve to carry into your daily work and activities the equanimity of solitude. Make a careful plan for your personal guidance, and try to live up to it under all circumstances.

Conserve your mental and physical vitality as you would your bank capital. Large reserves are necessary to large enterprises.

Stores of strength will give you confidence born of power.

JULY SEVEN

Be Faithful to Your High Trust

A complete philosophy of life is comprised in three gospels: The Gospel of Christ, the gospel of hard work, and the gospel of good cheer.

Live strictly up to these three gospels in your every-day life and you will get the best that is possible in this world.

The first is as enduring as eternity, the second brings certain reward, the third confers health and happiness, and the three combined yield the only true success.

Study these three gospels carefully, realize their vital importance, and make them significant factors in your personal life.

Appreciate your opportunities for self-development and service to others.

And remember that the crowning glory of achievement awaits everyone who performs his work faithfully to the end.

JULY EIGHT

Accumulate Reserves of Power

Fully realize that worry, resentment, resistance, and nervousness are destructive and disintegrating influences, and you will wish to eliminate them from your life.

To accumulate great reserves of physical vitality, it is necessary to avoid all undue nervous strain, tension, and excitement. Hurry, worry, and anxiety tend to defeat the object in view.

The best results are secured by a uniform attitude of poise, calmness, and self-control.

Several times a day consciously relax your mind and body. Then give yourself a silent or audible treatment of positive affirmations.

Confidently assert your right to health, harmony, and happiness.

Resolve that under all circumstances you will maintain a mental attitude of poise.

JULY NINE

Fortune Favors the Forearmed

Ordinary abilities, coupled with application and perseverance, often achieve extraordinary results.

Fortune favors the forearmed. It is wonderful how the most serious problems and difficulties are solved through earnest and painstaking industry.

The lives of the world's greatest men are records of incessant and intelligent effort.

The power of perseverance is incalculable. It is an obvious truth that you do not know what you can do until you try.

It is equally true that you cannot adequately estimate the great fields open to you until you have ascended the heights for advantageous observation. The capacity for hard work is an element of genius.

There is really nothing too great for a highly courageous mind.

JULY TEN

Persevere Towards a Great Ideal

The practical work of life demands constant and intelligent effort. Men who depend solely upon good luck or random chance to attain success are usually disappointed.

There is a large element of happiness in the discipline which comes from conscientious labor. The fine qualities which are recognized as essential to successful business are of great value in the social and other spheres of human intercourse.

The world tacitly condemns the man of idleness, and confers its highest honors upon the indefatigable worker. Indolence is degrading, while industry is elevating.

To take an active part among the world's workers is an honor in itself.

One of the richest gifts of life is the desire and ability to work diligently and earnestly for a great ideal.

JULY ELEVEN

The Value of Cheerfulness

Cheerfulness is a tonic for the mind and body. It has a directly beneficial influence upon the blood, nerves, and physical organs.

Cheerfulness is a valuable business asset. It is one of the greatest forces in winning and keeping friends. Cheerfulness, the co-partner of optimism, radiates confidence and enthusiasm wherever it projects its penetrating power.

Cheerfulness is the antidote to worry, fear, discouragement, perplexity, and discord. Cheerfulness gives mental alertness, serenity of mind, and broadened sympathies.

Cheerfulness brings contentment and tranquility, safeguarding its possessor from inordinate ambition, and the mental strain of haste and anxiety.

Daily affirmations of cheerfulness build life and vigor.

JULY TWELVE

Develop Your Superior Qualities

It is instructive to study the people around you, to talk with them, listen to them, and to form your silent estimate of their ways and characteristics. But just as you analyze and study other people, they do the same with you.

Hence the importance of developing your superior qualities, and giving them spontaneous expression in your daily life.

The world is passing silent judgment upon you, and every word you utter, every expression of face and body, every mannerism, habit, and mood, is contributing its share, however small, to the total impression you are making upon others.

Be careful, therefore, about your ways, sayings, opinions, manners, habits, and personal characteristics, that you may have the approval of your fellow men.

JULY THIRTEEN

With God All Things Are Possible

God is love. God is a spirit, and they that worship him must worship him in spirit and in truth. With God all things are possible.

The eternal God is thy refuge, and underneath are the everlasting arms. Trust in the Lord with all thine heart, and lean not unto thine own understanding. In all thy ways acknowledge him, and he shall direct thy paths.

The steps of a good man are ordered by the Lord: and he delighteth in his way. Be of good courage, and he shall strengthen thine heart.

Be careful for nothing; but in everything by prayer and supplication, with thanksgiving, let your requests be made known unto God.

And the peace of God which passeth all understanding, shall keep your heart and mind through Christ Jesus.

INSPIRATION AND IDEALS

JULY FOURTEEN

Cultivate the Habit of Listening

Listen and learn. Your mind must be quiet and receptive if you are to appropriate the best thoughts of other people.

It is impossible for you to generate and develop great ideas within your own mind while you are in a state of constant activity and expression.

When you listen attentively and mediate much, you will learn most from others and give your own thoughts opportunity to mature.

There are many persons anxious to speak, but only an occasional one willing to listen.

To be a good listener does not mean over-reticence, but simply the ability to be silently interested when occasion makes it desirable.

There are many blunders due to talkativeness, but few to taciturnity. What you do not say is not likely to do harm. Listen and learn.

JULY FIFTEEN

High Thinking and Right Living

Personal example of high thinking and right living is one of the greatest services you can render upon your fellow man.

Unconsciously you are influencing the lives of those about you, hence a deep responsibility rests upon you to make the most of yourself at all times.

The world's highly distinguished men have invariable set their light upon a hill where it illuminated mankind.

It is impossible to estimate the far-reaching effects of a useful, exemplary, consecrated life.

Take your lofty place in the world, and resolve that your daily example shall influence and inspire other men to great and noble purpose.

It is your profound privilege and duty to use your abilities and opportunities for the advancement of God's kingdom.

JULY SIXTEEN

Acquire the Habit of Giving

Acquire the giving habit. Give intelligently, freely, liberally. Give money, books, merchandise, counsel, sympathy, and inspiration.

Give something every day. Cultivate the giving habit as you do the saving habit. Give out of the fullness of your heart, not with the expectation of return or gratitude, but because it is right to give.

There is no greater joy in life than to render happiness to others by means of intelligent giving.

Never before in the world has there been so much generous, sympathetic and unselfish service. It is the spirit of the supreme giver, the Christ who gave His life that men might know the way to the Father.

You owe it to your highest self to give every day as you are able.

JULY SEVENTEEN

Cultivate Uniform Cheerfulness

It is a sure sign of greatness if you can rise cheerfully and confidently above a personal loss, misfortune, or disappointment.

However dark the present day may be, there is always the prospective sunshine of the morrow. Severe trial is often the most valuable discipline. Pain itself is a beneficent warning of nature that you should change some habit.

Sorrow sometimes seems to be only a grievous burden, yet many persons have emerged from it purified as if by fire. It is will to cultivate a philosophy of cheerfulness and healthy optimism to sustain you through times of inevitable trial.

You can find good in every person and circumstance, and you will be most likely to find that for which you look.

In seeking the good of others you will find your own good.

JULY EIGHTEEN

Choose Your Life Ideals

Dwell more and more upon thoughts of what you really want in your life. Close and hermetically seal the door of your mind against thoughts of what you do not want in your life.

You desire health, vitality, wisdom, peace, confidence, hope, friendship, harmony, independence, serenity, cheerfulness, happiness, success, culture, and righteousness.

Give your thought to these and kindred subjects, since dwelling upon them often and intensely tends to make them concrete in your life. Waste no thought upon things you do not want.

Do not worry about things you do not need. The power is yours to choose the ideals that shall daily possess and govern your mental life.

When your mind is right your life will be right.

JULY NINETEEN

Recognize and Use God's Thoughts

You are distinctly assured that in quietness and in confidence shall be your strength. There is to be no undue haste nor anxiety about your relation to God.

You are admonished to be quiet and fear not. As you daily connect yourself with the divine source of all love, truth, and goodness, you will learn to trust God absolutely for your guidance and protection.

The spiritual law is available to you now, and as you apply it in your daily activities you will be increasingly conscious of unlimited supply for all your needs.

The eternal mind of God is pouring forth a stream of perfect spiritual ideas for your enlightenment, protection, and happiness.

God's thoughts are yours in the measure that you recognize and use them.

JULY TWENTY

Concentrate Upon Essential Things

It is not the big blows, aimed full in the face, that hurt the most, but the little petty annoyances and worries that beat against us with daily regularity. They seem trifling and unimportant, but how they wound, and worry, and sometimes kill.

It is possible, however, to rise above annoyances and disappointments, by keeping the mind concentrated upon big, essential, fundamental ideas and purposes.

It is a fatal thing to brood over your troubles, most of which are usually imaginary. If today appears to you dark and unpromising, days of sunshine will surely follow.

Pleasure is enhanced by work, joy by sorrow, and success by seeming failure.

There is so much good work to do that you really have no time for worry and anxiety.

JULY TWENTY-ONE

Plan, Conserve, and Concentrate

Prudent planning prevents haste, waste, and inconvenience. When you have a work to do, an engagement to keep, an obligation to meet, or a service to render, prepare for it in ample time.

Provide for the possibilities of delay and disappointment. Some persons are in perpetual unrest because of haste and nervousness due to injudicious planning.

They do not allow themselves sufficient margin of time, too often leave things to chance, and have little realization of the brevity of an hour.

Anything done under nervous stress and excitement is almost sure to suffer in quality.

The best work is accomplished by men of poise and self-control, who have learned to conserve their personal force and to concentrate it for the most effective results.

JULY TWENTY-TWO

Develop Bigness of Daily Life

Your severest tests will come at times of emergency. Then the truth and stability of your beliefs will be put to trial. You believe in God as an ever available help in time of need, and that He has power to heal, protect, guide, and save you.

But an emergency arises – sudden illness, financial reverse, loss of friend, special hardship, national calamity – and then your real character is suddenly revealed in all its strength and weakness.

You are summoned to quick and definite decision. There will be disclosed the practical value of your beliefs and principles.

If you are equal to the test, your creed is justified. Think nobly and nobility will be manifested in your character.

Bigness of life is primarily bigness of spirit.

JULY TWENTY-THREE

Look to Spiritual Heights

Religion has to do with the refinement and ennobling of your best faculties. It seeks to raise you from commonplace, material things to spiritual ideals.

Surely it is only reasonable that you should devote some portion of each day to study and contemplation of things which are eternal and enduring.

Religion seeks to inculcate in you the divine qualities of love, humility, and patience, to bring you into consciously closer relationship to God, and to direct your steps toward spiritual heights.

All the truly great men of the world have been highly religious, for religion and greatness are practically synonymous.

As you study God's word, and apply His teaching to your daily life, you will experience a new and uplifting joy in all you do.

JULY TWENTY-FOUR

Confidently Leave Results to God

You will appreciate most that for which you work hardest. Fortunately the road to worthy achievement is neither smooth nor easy.

Decision, determination, discipline, courage, self-denial, and industry are pre-requisites to great success. There is an attractive power in a man of initiative and industry.

The world pays homage to the indefatigable worker. Men are drawn to him as to a magnet.

He develops self-confidence and self-respect, while he is at the same time winning the admiration of others.

Many of the most courageous men are those who work silently, systematically, and perseveringly, with no anxious thought about reward or recognition, content to do their work well and to leave the results to God.

JULY TWENTY-FIVE

Avoid Waste of Energy and Effort

We are all on Life's Stairway, going up or down, all going somewhere. And the people! Some are ascending, their faces radiant with sunshine.

Many others are climbing with faltering step and trembling heart. There are faces of arresting seriousness, and strong, honest faces that inspire weaker ones. So many thoughts need helping up. What a thrilling spectacle, a never-ending panorama of human beings traveling toward destiny. See those coming down.

A boisterous, careless, wild-eyed throng of pleasure-seeking, self-loving men and women. How fast they go! Two steps at a time and more – some are literally falling down.

Heedless, dissipated, selfish, ignorant, a seething crowd of unfortunate human beings traveling toward destiny.

JULY TWENTY-SIX

Realize Your God-given Powers

Your thought is your most valuable possession, and your immediate help in all difficulties.

Your personal achievement and ultimate success depend upon the kind and quality of your thoughts and the habitual way in which you think about yourself, your work, and your future.

It is principally through the use of your thought that you ultimately commit yourself to success or failure.

Realize more fully your God-given powers, your unlimited abilities, and your capacity for large development. It is not necessary for you to look outside for help, since you are a master in the making.

Resolve to make the most of yourself, to set your best thoughts to work for you, to think more highly of your abilities and possibilities.

JULY TWENTY-SEVEN

Be Conscious of Mental Growth

True progress means that you are daily growing stronger, better, and nobler, that you have an increasing desire for truth, justice, liberty, and righteousness.

You will be most conscious of mental growth at times of deep meditation, when thoughts of unsuspecting richness will come into clear view and urge themselves to be admitted into your active life.

Herein, too, is the value of prayer, since in the silent communication with the source of truth, your greatest powers are stimulated and brought into fuller realization.

Let no day pass without making it contribute its proper share to your development.

Your life should be one of steady, constant, definite advancement in knowledge, culture, and spiritual attainment.

JULY TWENTY-EIGHT

Think Daily on Spiritual Things

The divine teaching is explicit and emphatic, and he who runs may read: Bear ye one another's burdens, and so fulfill the law of Christ. Present your body a living sacrifice, hold, acceptable unto God, which is your reasonable service.

Lay up for yourself treasures in heaven, where neither moth nor rust doth corrupt, and where thieves do not break through nor steal: for where your treasure is, there will your heart be also. Be not conformed to this world, but be ye transformed by the renewing of your mind.

The world passeth away, and the lust thereof; but he that doeth the will of God abideth forever.

Blessed is the man that trusteth in the Lord, and whose hope the Lord is.

He that overcometh shall inherit all things.

JULY TWENTY-NINE

Good Work Speaks for Itself

One of the most insistent things in life is that you are ultimately judged by what you actually accomplish.

The busy world of workers gives scant attention to assertion, explanation, protest, apology, or complaint.

What counts most is not promise, but performance. Good work speaks for itself, therefore achieve something first, and talk about it afterward it you must.

Time spent in promises, regrets, and professions, is usually unavailing. The way to do things is not to dream about them, nor wish for them, but to do them. The distinguished men in all times have been prodigious workers, earnestly intent upon securing actual results.

The present age is intensely practical, and more than ever the race is to the alert, the energetic, and the industrious.

JULY THIRTY

Success is Making Right Choice

It greatly speeds your progress to know definitely and clearly what you wish to accomplish. It enhances your possibilities of successful achievement to know yourself, your abilities, and the difficulties you may have to overcome.

Many of the tragic failures of life are due to impulsive and ill-considered plans.

It is better to spend months if necessary in careful contemplation of a new project, than to plunge headlong into inevitable failure.

When you need outside advice, go directly to authorities. In an important enterprise take nothing for granted.

Prudent foresight will save you from many a disaster.

Success is often the result of right choices, rather than the possession of exceptional talents.

JULY THIRTY-ONE

Play to Win, But Play Fair

Play the game. Know the rules and observe them.
Always play fair, no matter what the other man may do.

Play to win. If you lose, be a good loser. But don't lose.
Study life as you would a game of chess. Know the moves, dangers, difficulties, and rewards.

Remember that no allowance is made for ignorance.
If you don't know the moves and rules, you must learn them through discipline and experience.

You must pay for mistakes. The game of life is intensely interesting, but to play it successfully demands constant diligence, patience, and alertness.

If your opponent cheats or falsifies do not imitate him. The real joy of the game comes from an innate sense of integrity.

Play to win, play hard, but always play honestly.
Play the game.

AUGUST

AUGUST ONE

Supreme Spiritual Counsel

It is more blessed to give than to receive. As you have opportunity, do good unto other men.

Give to the poor. He which soweth bountifully, shall reap also bountifully. Give alms of such things as you have. God loveth the cheerful giver. Every man shall give as he is able.

If your enemy be hungry, give him bread to eat; and if he be thirsty give him water to drink. Give and it shall be given unto you; good measure pressed down, and shaken together, and running over, shall men give into your bosom.

Every man according as he purposeth in his heart, so let him give, not grudgingly, or of necessity. Freely ye have received, freely give.

All things whatsoever you would that men should do to you, do you even so to them.

AUGUST TWO

Make Use of Every Opportunity

There is an eminent place for you to fill in the world. You cannot, however, rise higher than your thoughts and aspirations.

In order to reach the distinguished place which assuredly is possible, you must outline it definitely in your thought, dwell upon it frequently and intensely, and bend your best energies towards its realization.

The cardinal requirements for achieving and great enterprise are alert intelligence, untiring industry, and steadfastness of purpose.

Your progress largely depends upon having a receptive mind. Be eager to receive intelligent advice and suggestions for your personal advancement.

Listen patiently to advice or criticism, and try to apply it practically.

Make use of every opportunity for self-improvement.

AUGUST THREE

Obey the Best Impulses Within You

Keep the door of your mind resolutely closed against every undesirable, destructive, depressing thought.

Rise to the majesty of your personal power. There is a great place for you which you should claim by the sovereign right of your innate worth and ability.

Remember there is no altitude too high for your aim and aspiration. The great producers of the world have invariably been men of great vision, and greatness always looks upward.

As you daily develop increased power you will be the better ready for increased service. True greatness is expressed in love, reverence, honor, and nobility.

Obey the best impulses within you seeking expression.

Resolve to act promptly and energetically. Golden opportunities are now yours.

AUGUST FOUR

Your Own Will Come to You

Lift your eyes occasionally from your immediate work and take a long-range view of God's beautiful and inspiring creation.

Look away into the depths of the distant sky, and let your spirit find wing in the infinite.

Give your mind freedom to wander where it may in the immensity of space surrounding you. This mental excursion will bring you spiritual refreshment and many helpful ideas, so that you will return again to your regular duties with exaltation and new courage.

A flight of fancy is a desirable relief to concentrated effort. Never become so deeply absorbed in your work as to lose sympathetic touch with the world around you.

Be earnest, be strong, be true, and your own will come to you.

AUGUST FIVE

Be Clean in Mind and Body

The consciousness that you are clean in body and mind will enhance your feeling of self-respect. Bathe the entire surface of your body every day. Use water of a temperature to suit your needs. Use it regularly. Keep the pores of your body open by thorough daily cleansing.

Use pure castile soap and warm water. Finish with cold water, and rub your body briskly with the palms of your hands.

Self-massage is a beneficial exercise for imparting vigor.

Proper care of the body is vital to happiness. The consciousness of being clean will increase your confidence.

It is your duty to be physically and spiritually pure. Health and goodness are inseparable.

A clean mind and a clean body are essential to good work and a good life.

AUGUST SIX

The Remedy for Discouragement

There is great value in the power of concentration, yet you should be careful not to apply yourself too exclusively and continuously to one kind of occupation.

Unless you have interests outside of your routine work, your mind and life will become narrowed, and later on you may find yourself in a rut from which it will be difficult to extricate yourself.

Paradoxically as it seems, it is the busy man, not the indolent one, who has the most time and inclination for outside varied interests.

Occasional change from your regular work will enable you to return to it with refreshed mind and body.

Often the best remedy for worry, irritation, weariness and discouragement is simply a change of occupation.

AUGUST SEVEN

Keep Your Mind Flexible

To learn to bend with the storm and let it pass safely over your head may require long study and application, but it is worth while. To bend readily is as difficult as to acknowledge frankly when you are in the wrong.

Flexibility means to hold not too rigidly to your own opinions, but to give others a chance to express their views.

A flexible disposition keeps the mind healthy and receptive, wins friends, placates enemies, and saves one from many of the shocks and jars of daily life.

Do not fret yourself unduly if your friend fails to meet his obligations to your promptly. Do not quickly condemn another because he does you an injustice.

Waste no time in anger or in tears because you have been misunderstood or maligned.

Cultivate flexibility.

AUGUST EIGHT

Give Simply and Intelligently

Be grateful for the joy of life. Be glad for the privilege of work. Be thankful for the opportunity to give and serve.

Good work is the great character-builder, the sweetener of life, the maker of destiny. Let the spirit of your work be right, and whether your task be great or small you will then have the satisfaction of knowing it is worth while.

Let each day witness to your generous giving, with no expectation of return. Give simply and intelligently.

Do not wait for great occasions on which to render special service, but remember that small giving may be true and helpful giving.

Consider that God has given so much to you, you cannot possibly give too much to others.

You can practice all the great virtues in small as well as in large things.

AUGUST NINE

Put Your Best Ideas to Use

Calm expression of opinion is more convincing than angry argument. Your rights end where your neighbors begin.

It is wise always to do your biggest half-day's work in the morning. Smile in the face of adversity and you will surely conquer.

One good idea put into execution is better than a thousand schemes locked in the brain. If you are careless in little thing you will probably be careless in big things.

It is better to be in doubt than in debt. If you would be considered clever, be silent and let your friends talk. Where there are high motives and growing interests, there can be no dark and dreary days.

Spend a few minutes frequently in meditation.

Deliberate, but don't procrastinate.

AUGUST TEN

Keep Your Mind Receptive

When your mind is receptive, all the world teaches you. Wherever you are situated, there is wisdom ready to disclose herself to you. The knowledge you desire most earnestly is the knowledge you will likely receive.

When you read the best books, you will have as the guests of your mind the best thoughts of the best men.

You choose the kind and quality of thoughts in your daily life by means of desire and your mental attitude toward the world around you.

The master thinkers and doers of all time are ready to serve you at your bidding. There is a feast of reason at which you can sit at will.

It is simply marvelous how much has been prepared for the nourishment of your mind and soul, which you can have for the taking.

AUGUST ELEVEN

Stepping-Stones to Better Things

The truly valiant man recognizes no such thing as failure. He regards mistakes, misfortunes, and misjudgments as practical lessons in wisdom and personal discipline.

Tho he does not accomplish the particular object in view, he thinks of it, not as failure, but as a means to a higher purpose.

The most successful men have used seeming failures as stepping-stones to better things. It is not failure but lack of earnest and continued effort which causes so many men to fall behind in life's race.

Men who seriously and diligently try without succeeding, are deserving of greater praise than those who succeed without trying.

It is well to remember that right effort, combined with industry and earnestness, will ultimately bring sure reward.

AUGUST TWELVE

Live Up to a High Standard

You resolve to live up to a high standard of personal conduct.

You resolve to be kind, dignified, confident, and worthy. But at the close of the day you are conscious of not having fulfilled the terms of your resolution.

Upon careful examination you find that you have omitted the special act of kindness, have been timid, possibly undignified, have talked much of self, and have done little to elevate yourself in the esteem of your fellow men.

Hence the importance of regular daily self-examination to discover your special needs and shortcomings.

To live up to a high standard requires persistent effort and vigilance. When you make a new resolution, fortify it will a still greater resolve to fulfill it.

Only fulfilled resolutions are valuable.

AUGUST THIRTEEN

Let Diligence Speed Your Progress

Never give way to inertia, weakness, or depression. Rouse yourself, stand up squarely and erect, take several deep breaths, then apply yourself diligently to some useful work.

There is a prolific waste of personal force because of uncertainty and indefiniteness. When you know your destination, you can better choose the most direct route.

Make definite, positive, discriminating choices, then go forward with confidence in results. Thinking, planning, and aspiring should be followed by definite, earnest, vigorous effort.

Set yourself a great task today and let the night bear witness that it has been accomplished.

Give all the time necessary in which properly to consider a plan, but once the decision is made let diligence speed your footsteps.

Inspiration and Ideals

AUGUST FOURTEEN

Listen Every Day to God

It is an inspiring thought to know that God is always present and therefore always available.

Dwell intently upon this sublime face until it becomes clear and real to your consciousness, and you will experience a sense of augmented confidence and power.

Affirm to yourself, over and over again, that God is real, present, immediately and always accessible to you, and that you can depend upon him with confident assurance at any moment of the day.

It is only reasonable that the power which made you can sustain you. It does sustain you.

Listen much to God and He will instruct you and show you the way in which to go. In the degree of your meekness and obedience he will guide you toward light, truth, and perfection.

AUGUST FIFTEEN

Eliminate Discord from Your Life

Things are great or small, important or trifling, by comparison. Most of your past worries proved insignificant or imaginary when measured with the great facts of life.

If you once form the habit of selecting and dwelling upon important subjects only, you will have neither time nor inclination for the petty worries which beset so many lives.

Anxiety, irritation, despair, fear and the like, are mental, and therefore must be destroyed mentally.

As you realize the folly of these habits, you will more diligently strive to eliminate them from your life. They are not only worthless, but a serious handicap in the race for success.

Think constructively, and doubtful and discordant elements will fall away from inanition.

AUGUST SIXTEEN

Larger Possibilities for You

Greatness of life is largely the product of definite purpose and lofty ambition. You must aim to do some one great thing with all your power if you are to stand on the heights of achievement.

When you have made a definite choice of a worthy life purpose, there will come to you a wonderful sense of increased power, and many influences will set to work for the sole purpose seemingly of aiding your progress.

The consciousness at the close of each day that you have made real and substantial advancement toward a great purpose will increase your courage, and larger possibilities will be constantly revealed to you.

And in this spirit you will surely learn that all really worth-while work must be in harmony with God, and that worthy work always has divine approbation.

AUGUST SEVENTEEN

Read for Knowledge and Culture

Be selective in your reading of daily news. You do not want a constant mental picture of the world's crime, disaster, and distress.

Direct your attention to the beautiful, encouraging, and ennobling. Read editorials that are constructive, informing, and inspiring.

Read for useful knowledge and mental culture. Do not read anything simply because you have to read something.

Better sit in quiet communion with your own thoughts, with your eyes closed, than to gorge your mind with evil, calamity, tragedy, and human depravity.

There are great projects, vital problems, new discoveries, and world questions which make interesting and profitable reading. Be selective in your choice of subjects.

AUGUST EIGHTEEN

Resolve to Great Things

Resolved that I will be an intelligent optimist, and will look for the best in everyone and everything.

Resolved that I will daily develop the habit of constructive thinking. Resolved that I will maintain a high standard of personal conduct at all times.

Resolved that I will cultivate courtesy, appreciation, deliberateness, integrity, and sincerity in my daily life.

Resolved that I will always speak well of other people, and if I know nothing good I will keep silent.

Resolved that I will frequently examine my character and conduct with a view to further self-improvement.

Resolved that I will daily conduct my thought so as to accomplish the best results from my abilities and opportunities, and thus direct my life to great and worthy purpose.

AUGUST NINETEEN

Cultivate a Liberal Viewpoint

There are many hundreds and thousands of different opinions and temperaments in the world, hence you must not be surprised if the world is often in disagreement with you.

It is not desirable that all men should think precisely alike, since it is sometimes the very conflict of opposing ideas that most clearly brings the truth into view.

When you recognize the necessarily wide diversity of opinion, you will not be too insistent in your wish to have others think as you do, but you will see the desirability of each person thinking out things for himself, and presenting his own views in his own way.

Thus all may contribute something which may help to a final solution of a subject and a clearer apprehension of the truth.

AUGUST TWENTY

Guard the Realm of Your Thought

New habits make new horizons. Silently and imperceptibly you are forming habits which will ultimately determine the degree of your happiness and success.

Closely guard the quality of your thoughts, that they may lead to right habits and thence to right living.

Recognize and use such supreme qualities as courage, faith, humility, loyalty, temperance, and integrity. Let these be an active force in your daily work.

Use your mental power in large ways for large ends. Simplicity, peace, poise, confidence, and happiness are products of a well-ordered life.

The most vital work you have to do is within the realm of your mind, since thought is the primary cause of everything you plan, attempt, and achieve.

AUGUST TWENTY-ONE

Be Prudent in Forming Habits

Be true to your best self, to your highest ideals and aspirations. It is not what you assert but what you think that determines your real place in the world.

Have the courage to pursue your innate high ideals, and presently men will come to your way of thinking.

Truth is a power unto itself.

The infallible power is yours to command and use, and in precisely the degree that you do use it will you be strong, confident, and noble.

As you daily develop and accumulate reserves of mental and spiritual power, you will be the better ready for the responsibilities, emergencies, and obligations of life.

Above all else, be prudent in forming your personal habits, since multiplied habits make character, and character makes destiny.

AUGUST TWENTY-TWO

Consecrate Yourself to Work

When your mental household is in good order, outward circumstances will be powerless to enslave or discourage you. Your present environment affords you ample opportunity for developing patience, concentration, and power.

The way you meet today's tests and trials, today's problems and responsibilities, is an unmistakable indication of what you would do under more favorable conditions.

Cheerful and conscientious fulfillment of present duties is the only certain way to promotional and enlarged personal power.

The qualities and abilities essential to supreme undertakings are developed first in small things.

Consecrate yourself wholly to your immediate work and duty, and the way will rapidly open to larger responsibilities.

AUGUST TWENTY-THREE

Put a Seal Upon Your Lips

Talkativeness is a pernicious habit.

The talkative person falls into many mistakes and misunderstandings, which a little judicious silence would obviate. Talkativeness exposes a speaker to the danger of blundering, exaggeration, and offensiveness.

It is a form of selfishness, tending to monopolize other people's time, and to tax their patience.

The remedy for talkativeness is to put a strict seal upon one's lips, coupled with a firm solution to cultivate a listening and receptive attitude of mind.

Eagerness expressing itself in talkativeness is a lack of self-control. The habit of talking too much is a common failing, and a prolific cause of error and disagreement.

There should be right balance between speech and silence.

AUGUST TWENTY-FOUR

Make Your Progress Sure

Devote your time chiefly to essential things.

Make common sense your constant guide. Cultivate the friendship of helpful, progressive, worthy people. Utilize the little spare moments, usually wasted, to improve your mind.

Develop clarity of judgment, dignity, seriousness, and a sense of the profundity of life. Try to make everything contribute to your physical, mental and spiritual progress. Rid yourself of every retarding thought, every undesirable acquaintance, habit, or other influence.

Make this day count in a significant way in advancing your highest and best interests.

Be eager to receive and apply helpful suggestions from any source.

Seek the guidance of God in your morning and evening prayer.

AUGUST TWENTY-FIVE

Daily Read Only the Best Books

The systematic reading of good books confers many valuable benefits. It affords useful occupation. It develops concentration, reflection, and other mental facilities.

It is an antidote for loneliness and discouragement. It promotes serious-mindedness. It gives inward peace and strength.

It imparts the pleasures of surprise, familiarity, sympathy, appreciation, expansion, and revelation. It inculcates the elements of true greatness.

A taste for literature is one of the greatest joys of life. You can cultivate it if you have it not. Select a great essayist and steep yourself in his thoughts until you have caught his spirit and purpose.

Keep a great book at your ready hand to read at odd moments.

Be a conscientious reader of good books.

AUGUST TWENTY-SIX

Study Words as Vital Things

Word-study is thought-study in symbol. As you ponder a series of well-chosen words, there will follow in your mind a train of beautiful and inspiring ideas.

Words and thoughts are interactive and reciprocal.

You cannot study one without the other. As you dwell upon great and lofty words, corresponding thoughts will arise in your mind.

Observe the effect of expressing aloud a list of such words as honor, faith, rectitude, constancy, purity, integrity, conscientiousness, chivalry, liberality, loftiness, heroism, magnanimity, sublimity, altruism, and nobility.

Helpful ideas will at once spring to mind, and you will have an intensified desire to do something fine and enduring.

Words, like thoughts, are vital things.

AUGUST TWENTY-SEVEN

Grow Daily in Simplicity

Keep your life simple and sincere. Cultivate the graces of goodness and gentleness. Simplicity is the best and truest kind of greatness.

The simple life is strong, useful, and productive. It combines confidence with lofty purpose. Nature is simple in all her ways. The greatest things in life – beauty, love, truth, nobility, and righteousness – are simple in character.

Begin each day with a sincere desire to be strong and simple. Make simplicity the keynote of your aims and achievements.

Beware pride, selfishness, and inordinate ambition.

Liberality and serenity of mind come largely from a sincere desire to be simple.

As you grow in simplicity, your life will become full and beautiful, and you will be a constant inspiration to your fellow men.

AUGUST TWENTY-EIGHT

The Present Day is Yours

There are many fine things which you mean to do some day, under what you think will be more favorable circumstances.

But the only time that is surely yours is the present, hence this is the time to speak the word of appreciation and sympathy, to do the generous deed, to forgive the fault of a thoughtless friend, to sacrifice self a little more for others.

Today is the day in which to express your noblest qualities of mind and heart, to do at least one worthy thing which you have long postponed, and to use your God-given abilities for the enrichment of some less fortunate fellow traveler.

Today you can make your life big, broad, significant, and worth while.

The present is yours to do with it as you will.

AUGUST TWENTY-NINE

Live Up to a High Standard

Keep your head up, shoulders back, chest high, and spine straight. Be alert, cheerful, all-alive.

Fill your mind with happy, helpful, hopeful thoughts, so that these attractive qualities will be unconsciously expressed in your face, voice, and speech.

Cultivate the society of congenial people, and surround yourself with pleasant objects. Make every day definitely and distinctly contribute to your advancement.

Welcome to your mental household everything that is fine and beautiful. Turn resolutely away from the unlovely and undesirable.

Take your definite stand toward the world and compel others to ascend to your plane. Having chosen a high standard, live up to it strictly and conscientiously.

Never sacrifice principle for power.

August Thirty

Justify Your Spiritual Birthright

Every noble thought is stamped with immortality.

Every good desire is a promise of what can be. Every high aspiration is an intimation of possible achievement.

Let the controlling motive of your life be to do the will of God and to serve Him in sincerity and truth.

Then there will be revealed to you, gradually and surely, a great and holy purpose for which you have been equipped.

As the light of true spiritual knowledge illuminates your mind, the darkness of doubt will disappear, and you will become conscious of new and wonderful power.

The source of true happiness is not to possess but to serve.

Be resolute in your desire for truth and righteousness, and thus justify your spiritual birthright.

AUGUST THIRTY-ONE

The Sky Gives Perpetual Pleasure

The sky offers constant opportunities for spiritual enrichment. A clear blue dome suggests thoughts of purity and perfection. The fleecy clouds, moving with matchless grace and gentleness, remind us of the transient and unsubstantial.

The noontide of golden sunlight tells of God's fullness of love. Evening twilight gradually enfolds the earth in its soft shades, soothing the spirit and invoking silence.

Then comes night, and the star-studded sky rains down its countless lights upon all mankind alike. The study of the sky, with its wonderful panorama of color and beauty, exalts the mind and satisfies the spirit.

All day long the miracle is there for contemplation, and at night the eternal wonder is renewed, bringing peace and contentment.

SEPTEMBER

SEPTEMBER ONE

Go Directly to God for Your Needs

Your life is constantly subject to the law of cause and effect. What you think and do today determines largely what you will be doing tomorrow.

Confidence in an abundance of material possessions, of health, happiness, and success, tends to make these things concrete in your life.

As you think from day to day so will your life be. Keep your mind receptive to God's thoughts, and they will flow into your consciousness with fullness and illumination.

The eternal mind of God is constantly available to you. Go directly to God for your supply of good, and it will meet all your needs.

It is your inestimable privilege to use God's infinite ideas which He gives you in exact proportion that you are willing to receive them.

SEPTEMBER TWO

Cheerful Work is a Mental Tonic

Do the duty of each moment to the best of your ability, and be confident about ultimate results.

Cheerful work is a mental and physical tonic. There is inestimable advantage in approaching a difficult task with faith and expectation.

The spirit in which you do your daily work largely determines the quality of the results. Make yourself equal to every situation by vigorous and enthusiastic application of your best powers.

As you master small things you pave the way to larger achievements.

Whatever you do, do it well, since good work is its own reward. Find out your supreme talent and put it to work at a supreme task.

Launch yourself upon a noble enterprise which shall ultimately round out your life into worthy success.

SEPTEMBER THREE

The Truth Shall Make You Free

Love the truth. Buy the truth, and sell it not; also wisdom, and instruction, and understanding. The judgment of God is according to truth. His truth shall be thy shield and buckler.

The truth of the Lord endureth forever. Ye shall know the truth, and the truth shall set you free. The Lord giveth thee wisdom; out of his mouth cometh knowledge and understanding.

A wise man will hear, and will increase learning; and a man of understanding will attain unto wise counsels.

When wisdom entereth into thy heart, and knowledge is pleasant unto thy soul, discretion shall preserve thee, understanding shall keep thee.

Stand, therefore, having your loins girt about with truth, and having on the breastplate of righteousness.

SEPTEMBER FOUR

Cultivate Purity of Mind

Make your life harmonious by thinking only harmonious thoughts. Resolutely shut your mental door against all contrary ideas. Keep your mind inviolate.

Make your life beautiful by looking only at beautiful things. The world about you is wonderfully attractive, and you can deliberately choose what subjects shall engage your attention.

Make your life pure by cultivating purity of heart. To the pure all things are pure. Moreover, purity of mind builds bodily health.

Keep your life simple by conforming it to simple tastes, desires and habits. Simplicity is a safeguard against many of life's disappointments.

Keep your life righteous by studying God's truth every day, and by implicit obedience to your own conscience.

SEPTEMBER FIVE

A Suggestion for Daily Prayer

Pray thus: Heavenly Father, I thank thee for the privilege of prayer. I thank thee for the revelation of thy truth by which I am enabled to escape from all error in degree in which I am willing to receive and apply thy truth.

I thank thee for thy love which has always sustained me and will always sustain me in the proportion that I trust thee. I thank thee for life and opportunity which thou hast given to me that I may serve thee.

I want to know thy will, and to consecrate myself to good work. I want my life to fit in with thy great plans. Open my heart fully to thy love and law.

Bless me in every thought, word, and act, and may thy Kingdom come speedily to the hearts of all men.

In Christ's name. Amen.

SEPTEMBER SIX

Cultivate Poise and Self-Control

Learn to relax. Avoid all muscle strain. As you relax surrender yourself completely to gravitation.

When you sit, let the chair hold you. When you travel, let the vehicle carry you. When you retire, let the bed bear your entire weight. Rest and recuperation come through work done in repose.

Check all misdirected energy and wasted mental force. Right work energizes; strain incapacitates. Cultivate the important habit of doing one thing at a time with quiet deliberateness.

Always allow yourself sufficient margin of time in which to do your work well. Frequently examine your work methods to discover and eliminate unnecessary tension.

Aim at poise, repose, and self-control. The relaxed worker accomplishes most.

SEPTEMBER SEVEN

Build Well and Permanently

It is remarkable what can be accomplished with ordinary abilities when right desire is coupled with determination and diligence.

So-called drudgery and seeming disappointment are often forms of discipline leading ultimately to large success. Formidable difficulties will vanish before a courageous and indomitable spirit.

Many of life's greatest victories have been due to inexhaustible patience, resolution, and industry, rather than to extraordinary talent.

Daily self-discipline, and self-culture are essential to a highly progressive life. You are shaping your destiny by the quality and direction of your daily thought habits.

You are building well and permanently if you are taking instruction direct from God.

SEPTEMBER EIGHT

Your Personality Proclaims You

You attract to yourself the things you most fervently desire. Your home environment is an externalized expression of your mind.

Your outward appearance is a testimony of your personal taste and judgment. Your face reveals the evidence of your daily thought habits.

The tones of your voice reflect your disposition and qualities of heart. The words you use tell of the kind of books you feed your mind upon.

Your choice of friends, amusements, hobbies, and pastimes, indicates your power of discrimination.

Whether you know it or not, your personality is constantly expressing itself to the discerning world about you.

Take heed, therefore, and look well to the development of the finer voices within, that they may speak eloquently of you.

SEPTEMBER NINE

Your Influence Upon Others

What you are is quite as important as what you do. You cannot always be actively useful, but you can render constant service by your personal example.

Daily and hourly you are influencing the lives of those about you, and frequently you are doing greater and more enduring service because of your intrinsic character and personality than you would by admonition, suggestion, and preaching.

It is imperative to greatness of manhood that you cultivate right intention as well as right conduct.

Be assured that when you sincerely intend to be strong, gentle, pure, and good these qualities will naturally manifest themselves in your outward personality.

Greatness and goodness are fundamentally of the mind and heart.

SEPTEMBER TEN

The Infinite Source of Truth

Carefully observe the ill-effects of ignorance, fear, and superstition, upon the lives of many people around you, and you will see the follow of allowing these things to limit your own life.

Think deeply of the enslaving power of erroneous and misdirected thought, and there will rise within you a determination to be an earnest seeker of the truth.

Persistently hold in view the wish to know the truth, and it will gradually be made manifest to you.

Seek and you will find. It is the law that desire must precede fulfillment.

Daily, earnestly, insistently, study the truth, that it may keep you free from ignorance, fear, superstition, and everything unlike God.

You must ultimately go to the Infinite Mind as the source of all truth.

SEPTEMBER ELEVEN

Earn Your Rightful Place

You are largely what you deserve to be.

To secure your rightful place in the world you must earn it through developed ability and hard work.

Honor and fortune come by right attraction. Men who have attained things worth having in the world have worked while others idled, have persevered when others gave up in despair, have practiced early in life the valuable habits of self-denial, industry, and singleness of purpose.

As a result they enjoyed in later life the ease, comfort, and success so often erroneously attributed to good luck.

There is no royal road to great achievement and distinction. To be great you must use great means.

Life's biggest prizes are awarded to the resolute, valiant, and indomitable.

SEPTEMBER TWELVE

Learn from Every One You Meet

Education is not mere book-learning, but the culture of mind and heart. Education is knowing the most useful things, and doing them.

Education is the harmonious development of all the \faculties, and the bringing into view every virtue and perfection.

Your education does not end at school, but continues through life. You are forever a student.

You can learn from everyone you meet. Books, friends, nature, meditation, and travel are vital means to knowledge, discipline, and education.

What you know, makes you what you are. The riches of literature, science, art, philosophy, history, and religion, are yours for the taking.

Education is free, and the development of personal character is its crowning work.

SEPTEMBER THIRTEEN

Be Ready for All Emergencies

The best planned life has its daily problems to solve.

A spirit of patience and sacrifice is necessary to meet the recurring duties and difficulties which beset the daily path.

You have your obligations to friends and society, when often you would choose to be alone.

Perhaps bodily fatigue assails you before a task is completed, yet you must persevere to the end.

Untimely interruptions, distracting sounds, or intruding influences may severely tax your temper, but your duty is clear and you must bear all things with equanimity.

So that while it is right to plan for a life of uninterrupted harmony and happiness, you should so develop the qualities of patience and sacrifice as to be ready for all possible emergencies.

SEPTEMBER FOURTEEN

Plain Living and High Thinking

Genuine simplicity of life does not mean lack of aim, ambition, effort, and enthusiasm.

It means the foregoing of certain elaborate comforts, luxuries, and useless things which many short-sighted people think are essential to happiness.

It learns to do the right and desirable thing spontaneously. True simplicity contents itself with the fine, beautiful, substantial things of life.

It prefers to work quietly and unostentatiously, with no desire for inordinate riches, social prominence, or the applause of the multitude.

Simplicity squanders no time over trifles, baubles, and follies.

Simplicity concerns itself particularly with plain living, high thinking, and useful service.

SEPTEMBER FIFTEEN

How to Render True Service

Play your part in the warfare against evil, ignorance, and greed, by eliminating these factors from your personal life.

Public opinion is the aggregate of individual opinion. What you think, what you say, how you act, in your private capacity, is having its due effect upon the common welfare.

You influence the world for good as your practice simplicity, kindness, nobility, integrity, and generosity in your daily intercourse with men.

You render true service, and hasten the brotherhood of man, whenever you discountenance and discourage sensationalism, costly luxuries, undue excitement, and the feverish quest for money.

Simplicity and sincerity are divine qualities, leading to fineness and beauty of life.

SEPTEMBER SIXTEEN

You Can Achieve a Great Purpose

Success really means worth-while achievement.

It means undertaking a distinctive work and completing it.

In the ordinary sense it means a high degree of worldly prosperity. The money aspect of success should have due consideration, but no more.

Money is necessary, useful, essential, but it is only one element in true success. In the highest sense, success implies that you have actually attained some great purpose; that you have made judicious use of your thought, time, and abilities; that you have engaged in a worthy enterprise and accomplished it; that you have developed and rightly used your personal powers.

This is success in the truest and best sense, and it is worthy of your highest endeavors.

SEPTEMBER SEVENTEEN

Be Alert to Your Opportunities

Do not delude yourself with the belief that you would do better with larger opportunities while now neglecting smaller ones.

The qualities of initiative, diligence, and concentration are quite as essential in small as in large tasks. In doing small things well you are disciplining and preparing yourself for the larger opportunities to come.

One of the most fallacious ideas is to think you would do better work and make greater effort under other circumstances, while at the same time you are shirking present duties.

Be alert to the opportunities now at your ready hand.

Apply yourself with earnestness and intelligence to the work immediately before you.

Make the most of today's chances, and thus fit yourself for larger responsibilities.

SEPTEMBER EIGHTEEN

Cultivate the Power of Patience

Be patience in small as well as in large matters.

Be patient with people whose ideas and opinions differ from yours. Be patient when things do not terminate precisely as you wish.

Be patient toward those with whom you are in familiar daily contact. Be patient at all times and under all circumstances.

Patience manifests itself in a uniform evenness of temper. It enables you to listen attentively and receptively to others, even tho they interrupt and contradict you. Patience combines self-control with generosity, so that it bears easily with the defects, infirmities, and injustices of others.

Patience is an essential characteristic of all great and enduring accomplishment.

Patience is a power as well as a virtue.

SEPTEMBER NINETEEN

Make Right Use of Your Powers

The crowning gift of your success is the power it confers upon you to help others.

However easy or difficult you have found the road to achievement, having reached the goal you are in a position to point others the way.

So you should give generously of your experience, counsel, and even your money where it is desirable.

The test of the value of your success is the use you make of it. If it leads you to be selfish, indifferent, worldly, or egotistical, then it is neither worthy nor desirable.

It is said few men can survive prosperity, but there are many inspiring examples of successful mean who have used their success not for selfish satisfaction, but for the betterment of their fellow men.

These are the men who deserve success.

SEPTEMBER TWENTY

Do Everything for the Best

You can gain valuable instruction from observing the mistakes of the world about you.

There is wide-spread, self-assertion, envy, resentment, narrowness, pride, prejudice, and self-will. These are destructive elements, and always produce unsatisfactory results. Hence you will do well to take special means to keep such as these out of your own character.

As you develop yourself along lofty lines of thought and conduct, you will live above the common misunderstandings, dislikes, and discords of the world.

You will not be impatient to justify yourself in the eyes of others, but rather let your work and life speak for you.

You will not be in haste to rebuke faults and shortcomings in others, but with charity and forbearance interpret everything for the best.

SEPTEMBER TWENTY-ONE

Keep in Harmony with God's Law

The quest for happiness is a natural and worthy ambition. It is erroneous, however, to think of it as depending upon multiplied possessions, selfish indulgence, or unrestricted pleasures.

In all true happiness these is a large element of self-denial, restraint, temperance, and simplicity. Prerequisites to great happiness are a clear conscience, a pure heart, and an aspiring soul.

Happiness is in reality being in harmony with God's law. If you would be happy you must aim to live well, be grateful for your privileges, blessings, and opportunities, and regard happiness as synonymous with practical virtue.

It is still true that the virtuous are wise, the wise are good, and the good are happy.

Happiness is God-made; unhappiness is man-made.

SEPTEMBER TWENTY-TWO

Diligently Develop Your Abilities

Carefully scrutinize the lives of successful men, and you will observe that there has invariably been earnest and intelligent preparation for the success which followed.

Knowledge, efficiency, concentration, thoroughness, and similar acquisitions require long study and practice.

The only powers you can bring into use at a critical time are those which you have been developing, consciously or unconsciously, in advance of their being needed.

Success is not accidental but logical, the practical result of properly developed and applied abilities.

The hour or more you devote daily to diligent study, quiet meditation, and intelligent preparation, will play a vital part in determining the degree of your success when the supreme opportunity presents itself.

SEPTEMBER TWENTY-THREE

The Loveliness of Autumn Days

Gold and crimson autumn with her lap-filled treasures! Ripened days of departed summer.

Sweet and smiling season telling of accomplished tasks and victories won. Days of maturity and mellowness.

The brilliant colors of summer have given place to more somber tints. It is the time of softening lights, lengthening shades, variegated woods, lovely landscapes, and tranquil skies.

Earth, sky, and sea are transformed into new beauty, all nature joins in a conspiracy of rest, peace, and contentment, and at the close of the day the sun goes down in royal splendor of purple and gold.

Queenly autumn, in her many-colored robe, speaks eloquently of life, opportunity, growth, maturity, and transition.

SEPTEMBER TWENTY-FOUR

Be Master of the Situation

If you observe yourself frowning, let a pleasant thought smooth out your brow; if you discover yourself talking in a high key, deliberately lower the pitch of your voice; if you find your hands clenched, open them and let them drop to a dead weight at your sides; if you feel prompted to say something unkind, try the opposite plan of saying something pleasant and note the result.

To lose your temper is a sign of weakness. It never satisfies and is always harmful.

Once you realize the folly and disadvantage of a bad temper under any circumstances, you will take all possible means to safeguard yourself against it.

Slow to speak and slow to wrath is a good rule for daily guidance.

To be master of the situation you must first be master of yourself.

SEPTEMBER TWENTY-FIVE

Gladness is Akin to Goodness

Optimism is contagious. Cheerfulness promotes health and prolongs life. The good-natured man is a constant benefactor.

There is a sunshine of mind that defies and destroys doubt, disappointment, and discouragement.

Good humor is a tonic for the mind and body. Laughter is medicine for the soul. The intelligent optimist diffuses hopes, courage and confidence.

Gladness is akin to goodness. The world needs all the help you can give by way of cheerful, optimistic, inspiring thought, and personal example. Avail yourself of every opportunity to say a kind word, give an assuring smile, or extend practical help that will make some one hopeful and happy.

Intelligent optimism is one of the greatest constructive powers for inspiring men to great and noble purpose.

SEPTEMBER TWENTY-SIX

Form the Habit of Economy

You most appreciate the value of money when you need it most. So-called "good things," often turn out to be the "worst investments."

Save something regularly, however small, from your income. Every large fortune has its beginnings in small savings. The saving habit is a sure step to success and independence. The danger in a charge account is that you may over-buy. Prompt payment of obligations wins both self-respect and a good name.

There is something substantial about a man who has a bank account bearing interest. He has a feeling of security which must be experienced to be understood.

Saving does not necessarily mean discomfort, miserliness, or selfishness, but is a means to comfort, peace of mind, and prosperity.

Cultivate the habit of intelligent saving.

SEPTEMBER TWENTY-SEVEN

Have Faith in Your Future

Be done with the past, save where it serves to inspire you to greater and nobler effort.

Be done with regrets over vanished opportunities, seeming failures, and bitter disappointments, except in so far as they warn and safeguard you against their repetition.

Be done with the "might have been," and think of the "shall be." In all development, physical or mental, there are progressive stages, and what seemed to be failures, obstacles, and disappointments, were probably disguised opportunities for your ultimate good and advantage.

Let your motto be to look ever ahead, expectant of great things yet to come.

Trust God that no good is ever lost or withheld.

Direct your best impulses and inspirations to worthy work, with the assurance that all will be well with you.

SEPTEMBER TWENTY-EIGHT

Be Master of Your Own Mind

Every thought you think has an influence upon your life, great or small. All the thoughts you think are of two classes:

Constructive thoughts which build your powers toward useful ends, or destructive thoughts which deplete your resources. The thinking of most men is indefinite, haphazard, and negative.

They are frequently controlled by environmental, accidental circumstances, aimless newspaper reading, and other influences which tempt their thought away from constructive lines.

You can deliberately choose the right kind of thought you intend should govern your daily life. You can close the door of your mind against every undesirable, negative, useless thought.

You can be master of your own mind in the degree that you really want to be.

SEPTEMBER TWENTY-NINE

Be Loyal to the Will of God

However long you may experiment independently, you will at length realize you must harmonize your own will with the will of God.

There is no other way to eternal truth and happiness. It is exceedingly difficult for some men to conform strictly to God's laws, tho they know that His ways are necessarily best.

Human perversity insists upon trying its own ways first, and then, when it ignobly fails, turns to God and His divinely ordered laws as the only means to salvation and contentment.

To conform to God's laws is an indication of strength and intelligence.

True power and freedom come not through defiance of divine laws, but by willing obedience to them.

Be loyal at heart to the will of God and you can never go astray.

SEPTEMBER THIRTY

Seek the Truth at All Costs

Be diligent in your search for the truth. Hold tenaciously to the truth.

The more you appreciate the value of truth the more vigilantly will you guard it once you possess it. Give principal attention to fundamental truth.

Many problems which at first seem perplexing and difficult, are easily solved when carefully analyzed and traced to their source.

Truth is not usually complex, but simple. The more truth you acquire, the greater will be your capacity to grasp more and greater truth.

Study proofs rather that statements, essentials rather than incidentals. Apply yourself systematically and diligently to any problem, and the solution will be forthcoming.

The supreme quest of mankind is eternal truth.

OCTOBER

OCTOBER ONE

Divine Mind is Always Present

The realization that Divine Mind is always present and is ready to cooperate with you, will stimulate in you new faith, power, and purpose.

As you avail yourself to this great spiritual power, and use it in your daily activities, there will open to you unlimited possibilities of endeavor and attainment.

Today is the day for you to be renewed by the transforming of your mind, to make a new appraisement of your character and life.

The more you launch your thought upon a high spiritual plane, the more swiftly will your progress toward the ideal life. What you habitually think, you gradually become.

Seek constantly to make more of yourself and your opportunities.

Think, meditate, reflect, and then act with resolution.

OCTOBER TWO

Hints for Public Speaking

In your public speaking, don't hesitate, apologize, declaim, shout, fidget, clear your throat, or speak rapidly.

Don't be personal, sarcastic, funny, or violent. Don't speak in a high key, pace up and down, put your hands on your hips, or address the ceiling.

Don't speak through closed teeth, fumble with your clothes, over-gesticulate, nor wander from your subject.

Don't attitudinize, praise yourself, tell a long story, or rise on your toes. Don't emphasize everything, sway your body, stand like a statue, nor antagonize your audience.

Don't overlook the practical purpose of your speaking.

Don't do any of those things which you are quick to criticize in others.

And don't forget to sit down when you have finished.

OCTOBER THREE

Poise Confers Personal Power

Poise is power under control. Poise stores up energy and holds it in reserve for special use. Poise keeps you calm and deliberate under varied circumstances.

Poise does not mean weakness, vacuity, listlessness, nor indifference. Poise is strength, self-control, and reserve. Poise in its highest form suggests self-confidence, independence, and mastership.

Violence and vociferation eventually capitulate to poise. The man of poise rules. Work done in poise is best because it is thorough, painstaking, and intelligent.

Poise exercises a great influence over other men. It suggests immense stores of power in reserve.

Poise is power properly controlled and directed.

Poise conserves waste of vital energy, and gives balance to all the powers.

OCTOBER FOUR

Serve God in Your Daily Life

The inexplicable thing of life is that so many intelligent men deliberately and consciously barter the spiritual for the material, the eternal for the temporal.

The days of material man are as grass, as a flower in the field he flourisheth, the wind passeth over it and it is gone; yet many men continue to concentrate all their power and energies upon material riches, to the exclusion of the spiritual.

You are distinctly admonished to apply your heart unto divine wisdom, to have faith in God, and to do all to His glory.

This is your supreme duty and privilege, to serve God with all your mind and heart, to love your fellow man, to render Christly service whenever possible, and to submit yourself wholly to the divine will.

OCTOBER FIVE

Do Well Your Appointed Work Today

You can make your life a truly great and productive one, but it will require intelligent effort, rigid discipline, and a high and worthy aim.

All the distinguished men of the world have been earnest and prodigious workers looking for quality of results rather than for large reward.

Life without aim, aspiration, work, and achievement would be a monotonous treadmill. Indolence and idleness breed discontentment and carelessness.

To be happy you must work, and the greatest reward for your work is the consciousness that it has been well done.

The opportunities for useful work are abundant on all sides, and if you have the will the way will open wide to you.

Do your appointed work today and do it well.

OCTOBER SIX

Hold Yourself Erect at All Times

Don't slouch. Don't slump. Don't sag. Don't droop. Sit straight, stand straight, walk straight, think straight, talk straight, act straight.

Hold yourself erect and dignified. Keep your chest full and strong. Breathe deeply. Remind yourself many times during the day to expand your chest and keep it high.

Occasionally stand up, clasp your hands behind the back, bringing them well up between the shoulder blades, then take a full, deep breath, expanding the chest to its capacity, at the same time straightening the arms while keeping the hands clasped.

This is a splendid exercise for developing erect posture.

Correct carriage is essential to a strong and forceful personality.

Frequently check any tendency to droop. Stand erect.

OCTOBER SEVEN

The Solution for Your Problems

When you are in right relationship to God, all else will adjust itself correctly and harmoniously.

The precise counsel is to seek first the kingdom of God and his righteousness, and all these things will be added unto you.

That is to say, when you sincerely desire divine truth, and seek it with all your heart, it will answer all your questions, solve your problems, and satisfy your desires.

When your life is in strict conformity to the divine plan, you will want only what God wants you to have, therefore you cannot possibly be disappointed.

God is love, hence He wants you to have the wonderful things He has created for you, all of which are for your present good and ultimate progress into His Kingdom.

OCTOBER EIGHT

Seek Daily to Improve Yourself

Be not like those who remain mediocre all their lives rather than acknowledge their faults and shortcomings.

Be quick to recognize your own defects and to take prompt measures to remedy them.

Your best development depends upon your willingness and readiness to see your own limitations, and to plan intelligently for better personal means and methods.

If you are conscious of a fault in yourself, do not rest content until you have eradicated it.

If you feel there is some quality of characteristic which you should develop more highly, give your best efforts to that purpose.

It is your sacred duty to make the most of the powers that have been conferred upon you, and to develop yourself constantly toward a still higher standard.

OCTOBER NINE

Look to God for Guidance

The demands of the spiritual life are simple, but implicit.

To be true to your high calling, you must have a heart of humility and gratitude, a spirit of obedience and submission to divine authority, an honest principle of mind which causes you to look to God for guidance and approval, and a sincere desire to live a holy and devout life.

Anything less than this high standard of thought and conduct will keep you from your rightful place in the divine arrangement.

Stand, therefore, with your loins girt about with truth, having on the breastplate of righteousness, taking the shield of faith, and the helmet of salvation, and the sword of the spirit, which is the word of God.

Then will it be said of you: Well done, thou good and faithful servant.

OCTOBER TEN

Know the Purpose of Your Life

Cultivate a philosophy of your own. Study the meaning and purpose of life. Try to get clear ideas upon fundamental subjects.

Dwell upon the concept of God, his nature, will, and personality.

Meditate upon law and its marvelous power in the conduct of the world.

Give serious thought to such themes as divine love, the life and mission of Christ, the freedom of the will, the character and use of conscience, the doctrine of cause and effect, and the immortality of the soul.

Earnest study of subjects of this kind tends to enlarge the mind, broaden the vision, and inspire the heart.

Moreover, these subjects vitally concern your daily life, and the better you understand them the better you will be able to conform your life to the Divine purpose.

OCTOBER ELEVEN

The Sublime Story of the Sea

The sea is a sublime illustration of man's life.

Smooth, quiet, serene, it suggests tranquil and pleasant sailing.

But storms come, and wind and tempest threaten to destroy everything within their grasp.

Giant waves rise to awful heights, lightening flashes, and the great conflict of material forces strikes terror to the stoutest heart.

Then follows calm, the sea stretches out again in all of its gentle beauty and tranquility, and the voyager looks hopefully toward the desired haven.

You are now traveling over the sea of life.

Some days will be smooth, others stormy, but if you are intelligently equipped like the far-sighted mariner, you can be confident of a safe voyage and a friendly harbor.

OCTOBER TWELVE

Constantly Keep to the Right

When you walk along the street, keep to the right. When you ascend or descend a stairway, keep to the right.

When you are in doubt, keep to the right. When you know a course is wrong, keep to the right.

When temptation confronts you, keep to the right. When misfortune of prosperity comes to you, keep to the right. When men fail you, keep to the right.

When you feel discouraged, keep to the right. When the world misunderstands you, keep to the right.

When everything seems to go dead wrong, keep to the right. When you are perplexed and ready to give up, keep to the right.

When you think the worst has come, keep to the right.

Think right, act right, do right, and all will be right with you.

OCTOBER THIRTEEN

The High Purpose of Ambition

The supreme object of life is not satisfied desire, realized ambition, acquisition of personal power, accumulation of riches, nor indolent ease, freedom and contentment.

Life is activity, planning, dreaming, aspiring, doing, serving, pressing on from one attainment to still greater heights.

It is right and worthy for you to plan for a time when you can have respite from business or other regular occupation.

Such leisure is not for idleness, however, but for reading, writing, traveling, public speaking, or other useful forms of activity.

A fully realized ambition, with no hope nor desire for anything greater, would mean disintegration and death.

If you would be happy, keep your daily life filled with useful and interesting work.

OCTOBER FOURTEEN

The Value of Definite Purpose

Set before yourself a great and definite life purpose. Hidden away in your inmost soul is a transcendent ideal capable of realization.

What you need is not more capacity or greater opportunity, but increased resolution and concentration. Nothing will give you so much pleasure as the consciousness of making daily progress toward a great life purpose.

As you realize your steady growth in moral and mental strength, you will experience a new and wonderful desire to be something and do something worth while in the world.

There is no greater fallacy than to think you will surely do at some future time the better things you are capable of doing now but neglect to do.

Good intentions long deferred lose their vitality.

Arise to a realization of your rightful possessions.

OCTOBER FIFTEEN

The Lessons of Experience

Experience should bring restraint and repose.

When you have a sense of life's values, you will not indulge in hurry, anxiety, restlessness, or fear. Matured judgment will make you realize that the best results come from easy, confident, deliberate effort.

The best work is done in poise. Efficiency brings ease, certainty, and self-assurance.

Combined experience and efficiency will enable you to achieve results without waste of time or energy. In all departments of human activity, the man of matured judgment and self-control is likely to be master of the situation.

The special reward of discipline and diligence is that they give an intelligent view of life's values, and show you how to get the best results without undue strain.

OCTOBER SIXTEEN

A Big Place for You in the World

There is a big place for you in the world. The measure of your ultimate success will be the measure of your faith in yourself and the realization that you possess inexhaustible personal resources.

This is the day of big things. The insistent demand is for men of initiative, self-confidence, resourcefulness, and efficiency.

Modern business is touching the secret springs of men's powers, and galvanizing into actual use many new ideas and personal forces.

Reconstruction is going on apace, and greater efficiency is demanded than ever before.

Great unseen forces are at work, powerful, silent, subtle, significant, impelling men to build for larger usefulness.

There is a big place for you in the world, and you can fill it if you will.

OCTOBER SEVENTEEN

Make Your Life Acceptable to God

Let no influence tempt you to swerve from the chosen path of truth and righteousness.

Give freely of your time, thought, money, and influence, that others may profit by your life and example.

Keep always before your eyes the ideals of truth, beauty, and holiness. Be faithful to that which you know to be right. Take your stand today on the side of God.

It is a commendable thing to do justly toward all men whether they do likewise toward you or not. You are required to do only that which you have power to do, therefore plead no excuse of impossibility.

Do not longer defer your good intention to make your life more acceptable to God.

Today is the time to be doing. Your soul is in the making here and now.

OCTOBER EIGHTEEN

Plan a Course of Great Reading

In one hour a day, for a period of one year, you can read the best that has been said by such writers as Plato, Aristotle, Marcus Aurelius, Epictetus, Plutarch, Shakespeare, Milton, Bacon, Carlyle, Ruskin, Macaulay, Newman, Washington Irving, Lowell, Hawthorne, Emerson, and Thoreau.

A carefully planned course of reading of the best authors will, in that comparatively short time, give you the essentials of a liberal education in classical and modern thought.

Read Addison for clearness, Lamb for simplicity, Bacon and Emerson for epigram, Carlyle for ruggedness, and Ruskin for rhythm and word-painting.

Read for knowledge, creative power, satisfaction, and relaxation.

A love for great literature is one of the noblest pleasures of life.

OCTOBER NINETEEN

Resolve to Do Constantly Better

The best medicine for discontent and discouragement is useful occupation.

You are in the world to make something of yourself, to develop your powers and abilities for worthy use, to render substantial service to your fellow men.

A well-planned life has no room nor inclination for useless worry and dissatisfaction. Every minute of the day is significant to the earnest and ambitious worker.

Life is rich with opportunity, as you elect for yourself every morning whether the day will be fruitful of results or not.

Plan a program of practical usefulness for each day, fill up the hours with interesting work, resolve to do constantly better, and you will find your life steadily expanding into beauty and joyousness.

OCTOBER TWENTY

Cultivate Uniform Self-Control

Never send a letter written in anger or resentment.

If you write such a letter in order to relieve your pent-up feelings, or to express righteous indignation, put it on your desk for twenty-four hours, and upon deliberate reflection you will destroy it.

Anger in any form is weakness, but put in writing it remains on record to stand forth an accusing witness against your better self.

Resolve never under any circumstances to write an unkind or ill-tempered letter, nor to place on record anything which you could by any possibility live to regret.

Make it a rule never to say anything in anger. Boys draw in their kites at will, but you cannot annul the spoken word.

Think well before you speak.

OCTOBER TWENTY-ONE

Make Your Life Happy and Fruitful

As you daily give your mind and heart in homage to God, and acknowledge Him as the guide of your life, you will grow toward spiritual perfection.

Tho a task seems slow, you will do well to persevere, since work is the remedy for all the worries and discords which burden men.

Carefully analyze, develop, and apply in your daily life, the following spiritual qualities:

Charity, compassion, courage, devotion, faith, humility, integrity, justice, kindness, love, nobility, patience, piety, purity, repentance, reverence, righteousness, self-control, self-denial, sincerity, sympathy, temperance, tolerance, truthfulness, and unselfishness.

Practical use of these qualities will tend to make your life happy and fruitful.

OCTOBER TWENTY-TWO

Keep Your Mind Filled with Good

There are subtle forms of evil which you should guard yourself against as you would against disease and pestilence.

When you feel toward others the first intimation of resentment, envy, contempt, or discontent, annihilate the thought on the instant. Drive it out of your mental world and be done with it.

As a great growing personality you should be eager to discover and destroy any weakness in yourself.

Let thoughts of appreciation, admiration, approval, gratitude, and generosity be uppermost in your mind.

The best antidote for evil of any kind is to keep your mind filled with good thoughts and your life occupied with good works.

As you ascend in your thought, you will find yourself in a new world of beauty and usefulness.

OCTOBER TWENTY-THREE

Seek the Best in Everything

Look always for the pleasant, the beautiful, and the constructive. Life is too precious to be frittered away on useless, negative, depressing things.

Cultivate a spirit of appreciation and gratitude. Seek the best in everything. Be thankful for the privilege of life.

Think highly of those about you, and give them the benefit and encouragement of your most generous thoughts.

Your mental habits have a vital influence in shaping the character and productiveness of your daily work.

Confidence and belief in your own ability to achieve will speed your progress.

Your mind is a wonderful workshop, in which you plan, systematize, devise, invent, and picture ideas which are subsequently to be expressed in material form.

OCTOBER TWENTY-FOUR

Difficulties Are for Discipline

Rely upon your own resources. You have within yourself all the power necessary for a useful, progressive, successful life.

Pluck and perseverance are the handservants of prosperity. Difficulties are for discipline. Problems promote progress. Right results and rewards come from labor, not luck.

Apply the abilities you now have and your powers will develop in the use. You are now living in a time of most wonderful opportunity, with practically no limit to your possibilities of growth and usefulness.

Mighty influences within and without are at your command.

You may now decide for yourself what you will do with these immense resources, and whether you will take a place among the successful man of your day.

OCTOBER TWENTY-FIVE

Faith Makes All Things Possible

Have faith in God. Walk by faith. Faith is counted for righteousness. Faith without works is dead.

Without faith it is impossible to please God.

Fight the good fight of faith, lay hold on eternal life. Faith is the substance of things hoped for, the evidence of things not seen.

Take the shield of faith, wherewith ye shall be able to quench the fiery darts of the wicked.

Draw near with a true heart in full assurance of faith. If thou canst believe, all things are possible to him that believeth.

He that cometh to God must believe that He is, and that He is a rewarder of them that diligently seek Him.

Be able to last say that you have fought a good fight, have finished your course, and have kept the faith.

OCTOBER TWENTY-SIX

Use Today's Opportunities Today

Every day you should plan, initiate, aspire, resolve, systematize, eliminate, concentrate, persevere, work, simplify, accomplish.

Life is made up of work and play, ambition and achievement.

You are responsible for the right use of your talents. The days pass quickly by, and the vital things you wish to do should be done with dispatch lest procrastination rob you of your opportunity and rightful reward.

Set your best powers to work today, that you may be able to say at its close that you have made conscious and substantial progress toward a great ideal.

There is so much possible to you that you cannot delay an hour without personal loss.

Make the best of today and its opportunities.

OCTOBER TWENTY-SEVEN

Cultivate Sunshine of the Mind

Get your enjoyment out of life daily and hourly as you go along. Do not wait on holidays and special occasions on which to give full play to your spirit.

Liberate your joy thoughts every day, extract constant happiness from your work, live in the mental sunshine now. Look for the bright things in men and life, interpret everything for the best, be an intelligent optimist.

Always see the bright side of the picture. Cultivate a sunny, hopeful, buoyant, attitude of mind. Seek those things which are cheering, inspiring, exhilarating.

Make the most of today's opportunities, cast away all thoughts of care, worry, and melancholy, and carry yourself in a mental attitude of genial expectation.

Cultivate sunshine of mind.

Inspiration and Ideals

OCTOBER TWENTY-EIGHT

Golden Opportunities Await You

Dare to originate, initiate, experiment, and explore.

Do not hesitate to venture into new fields of investigation and enterprise. The greatest discoveries are yet to be launched, the most eloquent sermons are yet to be preached, the highest achievements are yet to be realized in all departments of human activity.

There is a field of unlimited opportunity open to you, wherein you can have the widest scope of abilities.

Resolve today to choose a definite work, and to apply your best powers to it with energetic purpose.

Overwork is injurious, and a monotonous task is disheartening, but congenial, useful, productive work is the secret of mental and physical health.

Take immediate advantage of your golden opportunities.

OCTOBER TWENTY-NINE

A Place of Distinction for You

Your degree of success is not measured by what you say and promise, but what you attempt and achieve.

The world awards its prizes not for excuses and explanations, but for performance and results.

Intelligent men read you like an open book, and accurately appraise the kind and quality of your success.

The creative, planning, aspiring power within the realm of your mind, coupled with earnest application and industry, is sufficient to place you in the front rank of men.

Life is rich with opportunities and possibilities for the ambitious and persevering. Successful men in all departments of life have been characteristically hard workers.

There is a place of distinction for you, if you emulate the example of great men.

OCTOBER THIRTY

Increase Your Faith and Courage

Cultivate and encourage within yourself only those thoughts which you know will increase your faith, courage, determination, and other success-making qualities.

Think right and you will act right, and just as you think and act right you will be on the way to right results.

It is remarkable how a life that is ordinarily dull and unproductive can be changed by means of right thinking into a life of great and useful effort.

Wrong results in your life are primarily produced by wrong thinking, and the only way to annihilate wrong thoughts is to put right thoughts in their place.

Wherever you are at this moment, there is an incomparably higher place for you.

What you might have been, you can be.

OCTOBER THIRTY-ONE

Progress Toward a Great Goal

Daily drill and discipline are necessary to the formation of right habits.

Every man has undeveloped and unsuspected qualities in himself which can be cultivated in a marvelous way through systematic practice.

Timidity can be replaced by confidence, indolence by industry, aimlessness by concentration, and limitation by perseverance, all by means of daily exercise.

Self-control is a preeminent quality in ideal character and large personal success.

What most men need is vigorous training in self-discipline, self-control, self-respect, and self-government.

When a man has cultivated these qualities as unconscious habits, he may assume his rightful place in society, and feel assured that he is daily progressing toward a great goal.

NOVEMBER

NOVEMBER ONE

Always Listen to Good Counsel

It is worth while to listen to advice, since you always have the privilege of rejecting it if it does not meet with your approval.

Many persons are not amenable to suggestion, and thereby often lose valuable ideas. To decline advice openly and abruptly is imprudent and ungracious.

Much of the advice offered is sincere, emanating from kindness of heart and a desire to render helpful service.

It is often beneficial to know the other man's viewpoint, since his opinion may be based upon longer experience and better judgment than yours.

Cultivate a mind receptive to the generous counsel of others, give readily your ear to all suggestions intended for your advancement and improvement.

You can learn something from every one you meet.

NOVEMBER TWO

Every True Prayer is Answered

True prayer is cooperative. You cannot properly ask God to relieve you of responsibility.

You ask Him to make the way clear to you, to give you desire and diligence to labor, to endow you with power equal to your duties and obligations.

Prayer is not a substitute for personal effort. Your petition to God must first be right, followed by earnest and intelligent cooperation on your part. Every right prayer is answered, tho not always in the precise way you desire.

The immediate value of prayer is manifest in its regenerating and uplifting influence upon him who prays, but the larger effect of such prayer can be understood only by the omniscient God.

True prayer is receptive, cooperative, confident, and submissive.

NOVEMBER THREE

Build Only Desirable Qualities

There are negative, destructive, undesirable qualities, such as fear, envy, anxiety, resentment, anger, hatred, captiousness, incivility, contentiousness, egotism, irascibility, ingratitude, disrespect, disloyalty, selfishness, effeminacy, pessimism, cruelty, enmity, indiscretion, suspicion, vulgarity, and grumbling, all of which lead to depression, discord, and dissatisfaction.

There are positive, constructive, desirable qualities, such as faith, integrity, goodness, confidence, love, charity, appreciation, self-reliance, enthusiasm, sociability, integrity, sympathy, benevolence, tenderness, toleration, and adaptability, all of which lead to health, harmony, and happiness. You elect yourself to either of these classes of thinkers.

NOVEMBER FOUR

Good is a Direct Gift from God

Good is infinite, hence the supply can never be diminished nor exhausted. Good is inclusive, not exclusive.

It is for you and all others. It is impossible to monopolize it. It cannot be limited nor impaired. Good is the antidote for worry, fear, discouragement, anger, and temptation.

Substitute the thought of good for the thought of evil and the latter will instantly disappear.

Good is not something to be used occasionally, but is an available power for your use now and always. Good is one of the greatest gifts from God, whereby you can daily grow in love and righteousness.

Good is directly from God, since God is good.

As you express good, you express God.

Keep in close touch with God and your life must be good.

NOVEMBER FIVE

Make Wise Choice in Your Books

You need to have no dull hours if you are a sincere lover of books.

Should discouragement, sorrow, or difficulty assail you, it is your privilege to turn to a good book for inspiration, solace, and refreshment.

Books are ever available friends, ready to serve you at will. In reading, the vital thing is what you assimilate. It is possible to read omnivorously, yet acquire little in real knowledge and culture.

Method, judgment, and discipline are as important in the choice and reading of books as in the conduct of a successful business.

There is nothing that will precisely take the place of a taste for good literature.

To possess half a dozen of the great books of the world is to be rich in a great and enduring sense.

NOVEMBER SIX

Always Start Your Day Right

The manner of beginning the day is often left to chance. Yet it is of the most vital importance in fashioning and influencing the day's work.

Let your mind dwell upon distressing newspaper topics, or drift into discouraging thoughts, as a prelude to the new day, and it will affect you adversely.

Begin the day with an inspiring passage from a great author, or an uplifting thought from your own experience, and you will feel its effects in your subsequent activities.

It is the first thoughts of the morning which give color and character to the day's plans and work.

Be sure, therefore, always to begin the day by dwelling upon some ennobling and encouraging thought.

Use it as a keynote to the day's endeavors.

NOVEMBER SEVEN

Keep Right on with Your Work

It is comparatively easy to smile when blessed with friends, fortune and fame.

The supreme test of your real qualities, however, is when everything seems to be against you, when friends prove false, plans go wrong, illness overtakes you, and money, position, and those dearest to you are taken away.

If a reverse comes to you, look at it philosophically and keep right on with your work.

If a friend breaks faith with you, forgive the fault, and keep steadily to the main purpose of your life.

If a seemingly overwhelming disappointment assails you, rise to your full stature and keep on courageously with your chosen task.

If everything goes against you, don't give up, don't worry, don't falter, but smile and keep right on with your work.

NOVEMBER EIGHT

Acknowledge God in All Your Ways

Your sufficiency is of God. Nowhere else is it possible for you to find complete satisfaction and contentment.

You are transformed by the renewing of your mind and being filled with the fruits of righteousness.

Thus does God work in you both to will and to do of His good pleasure. You are not sufficient of yourself, for alone you could do nothing. You are wholly dependent upon the Divine Father.

Trust, therefore, implicitly in Him, and lean not on your own understanding. In all your ways, in every thought, aspiration and enterprise, seek and acknowledge Him, and He will direct you in the paths of truth, love and righteousness.

God is all, and as His divine creation you are privileged to participate in His bounty.

NOVEMBER NINE

Aspire to the Highest Things

Take your rightful place in the world. Think highly of yourself as having unlimited powers and possibilities.

Make yourself worthy of great and honorable success by right thinking, lofty aspiration, and energetic action.

Realize the tremendous unused resources at your ready command, and make every day contribute in a definite and substantial way to your personal progress.

Take courage and inspiration from the example of those successful men who first had to solve difficult problems and surmount obstacles such as sometimes confront you.

Always keep this clearly in mind: Today is the day to claim your birthright, to do your best work, to achieve all of which you are now capable, and to aspire to still higher things.

NOVEMBER TEN

Do the Most Important Things First

Waste no time on trifles and non-essentials. The daily squandering of a few minutes amounts in a year to many hours.

What principally differentiates the highly successful man from others is his discriminating use of time.

Cultivate a proper sense of values as applied to your daily interests and activities.

At the beginning of each day determine what are the essentially useful and valuable things for you to do.

Keep them clearly before your mind, and apply your best powers to their accomplishment. When possible do the most important things first and try to complete them.

Be sure that you are engaged in work worthy of your abilities, and that your best efforts are being steadily directed toward a great ideal.

NOVEMBER ELEVEN

Plan with Judgment and Foresight

Many persons give up just as victory is coming to them.

Many a failure might have been translated into success had there been a little more staying power.

Success is often just around the corner, and therefore very near tho it cannot be seen.

In the routine of the daily difficulties must be met, obstacles surmounted, problems solved, and sometimes seeming defeat must be looked bravely in the face.

But the man who is confident, heroic, determined, patient, and persevering, will ultimately win.

Hard work is the sovereign remedy for a weak will.

Have a definite daily purpose, plan with judgment and foresight, think intelligently, work diligently, and be assured that something fine and great awaits you further on.

NOVEMBER TWELVE

Be a Sincere Disciple of Truth

If your heart is daily growing great and generous, if you are taking increased interest in the common happiness of others, if you are earnestly endeavoring to fill the hours of the day with useful work, if you are frequently making earnest supplication to God for guidance and wisdom, then be assured you are progressing toward the kingdom.

The way to peace, happiness, and perfection has been implicitly pointed out to you.

You are to practice humility, serve and glorify God in your body and in your spirit, run with patience the race that is set before you, and let your light so shine before men that they may see your good works and glorify your Father which is in heaven.

The way is plain to every sincere disciple of truth.

NOVEMBER THIRTEEN

Set Your Mind Upon a Great Ideal

This day offers you new and inspiring opportunities for self-culture and personal progress toward a great ideal.

As you train yourself to discriminate between the important and unimportant, the true and the false, the beautiful and the ugly, the eternal and the temporal, you will see new and wonderful possibilities in the world about you.

Your daily life is made up of desires, choices, discriminations, judgments, and acts. These are under your personal control, so that in reality you are daily making your own destiny.

You set before yourself the goal which you wish some day to reach, whether it be high, low or mediocre.

Nothing can hold you back if you have set your mind and heart wholly and earnestly upon a great life purpose.

NOVEMBER FOURTEEN

Keep the Doors of Your Mind Open

Ignorance is a prolific cause of prejudice. What we do not understand, we are inclined to disbelieve.

When we want a thing to be true, we formulate all the available reasons for such a conclusion, and deliberately close our minds to opposite views. We are supersensitive about our opinions, and we are loath to acknowledge when we are wrong.

Opinions once formed take tenacious hold of the mind and are not easily dislodged, however erroneous they may be.

The only sure course for the lover of truth is to throw the doors of his mind wide open to receive all the possible light upon any subject in question. Breadth and liberality of mind can be secured only in this way.

Prejudice always shuts the door, but truth seeks an open field and no favors.

NOVEMBER FIFTEEN

Daily Study Inspiring Words

Repeat aloud and carefully study this list of inspiring words:

Achievement, ambition, aspiration, beauty, chivalry, Christ, confidence, conqueror, consecration, courage, determination, devotion, earnestness, efficiency, enthusiasm, eternity, faith, fame, fortitude, friendship, God, greatness, happiness, heaven, heroism, holiness, home, honor, ideal, immortality, invincible, justice, knowledge, liberty, life, love, loyalty, mastery, mercy, mighty, mother, nobility, omnipotent, omniscience, patriotism, peace, perfection, pluck, power, prayer, progress, prosperity, redeemer, rejoicing, revelation, righteousness, salvation, sovereign, success, supreme, sympathy, thanksgiving, triumphant, truth, victory, virtue, will, zeal.

NOVEMBER SIXTEEN

Regards Life as a Great School

The fine art of living is acquired only through long discipline, observation, and experience.

Day by day you have opportunities for correcting in yourself mistakes and misjudgments.

As you see where you might have done differently and better, you can record the item in your memory and resolve to profit by experience.

Life is a great school, in which you are constantly learning what to do and not to do, how to plan and execute better.

The schoolmaster may seem stern and relentless at times, but the discipline and instruction are for your ultimate good.

Study the lessons assigned to you in the wonderful school of life, and if occasionally a problem seems difficult, be assured a solution awaits you somewhere.

NOVEMBER SEVENTEEN

Keep a High Standard Before You

Set before yourself a high standard of personal dignity, and resolve to adhere to it strictly.

There are imprudent people who descend to foolishness, empty joking, undue familiarity, and airy persiflage, usually to their own serious undoing.

Politeness and pleasantness are not incompatible with dignity.

The deplorable habits of contentious arguing, aimless talking, and pretentiousness should be carefully guarded against. In every sphere of life it is the man of dignity who gains the greatest respect and confidence.

Set a high standard for yourself, and compel other men to come up at least to yours – never descend to theirs.

So will you surely develop a character that will stand the test of time.

NOVEMBER EIGHTEEN

Simplicity Tends to Happiness

Let simplicity govern your life.

The habit of constantly reaching out for something just beyond your grasp will tend to bring discontent rather than happiness.

It is destructive to your tranquility of mind to envy others what you have not, to want too many of the things you see around you, and to dwell overmuch upon your own desires.

Use and enjoy what you now have, be grateful for present opportunities and blessings, and trust your ability and the future to bring what is good and best for you.

True happiness does not depend upon great material possessions, but emanates largely from the mental qualities of contentment, confidence, serenity, and beneficence.

Simplicity of life always tends to happiness.

NOVEMBER NINETEEN

Put Your Life in Order Today

There is not a single trial, disappointment, worry, sorrow, or grievance in your life which cannot be turned to good purpose.

Whatever happens to you, whether it appears to be good or ill-fortune, offers a means of personal growth and advancement toward better things. The discipline of daily life is essential to true culture.

Begin each day with an earnest desire and a firm resolution to obey the divine will. God has provided everything good and beautiful for your highest happiness and welfare.

The work still to be done lies with you, in acquainting yourself with divine law and adjusting yourself to it.

There is inconceivable satisfaction in a life consecrated to God and His ways.

Set your life in order today.

NOVEMBER TWENTY

Let Your Good Habits Serve You

Work with enthusiasm. Cultivate laughter and good cheer. Be tolerant of other people's opinions. Constantly apply the Golden Rule. Have a daily play-time. Breathe deeply. By systematic and orderly in the details of your work.

Avoid the desire to set other people right and to reform the entire world. Aim to influence other lives for good by the force of your example.

Have a definite daily program. Avoid waste movements, such as foot and finger tapping, rocking, and nervous clearing of the throat.

Keep your mind constantly filled with wholesome, uplifting, healthful thoughts.

Be ready to adapt yourself to the unexpected and uncongenial.

Form good habits and let them work for you automatically.

NOVEMBER TWENTY-ONE

Stop Abnormal Haste and Strain

Learn to relax, and let go, to do things quietly and confidently. Cultivate cool-headedness, prudence, deliberateness, and self-control. Stop abnormal haste and strain.

Take the tension off your body by dropping it from your mind. View things in the right perspective.

Put a proper estimate upon your work and interests, but do not overestimate their value and importance.

Do everything with an inner sense of peace and poise.

If you have a fault in your character or method of working, which is retarding your best progress or holding you back from success, resolve at once to examine such fault, to face it fearlessly, and to take special means to eradicate it.

Growth in character depends upon intelligent elimination of correction.

NOVEMBER TWENTY-TWO

Cultivate Integrity of Mind

The habit of inflexible integrity confers many personal advantages. It gives a sense of self-confidence and independence which makes one equal to every circumstance.

Truth and duty have been watchwords of the world's greatest men, sustaining them through times of evil and good report.

When men know that your word is as good as your bond, and that nothing can swerve you from your chosen path of duty, you have one of the most valuable of personal assets. The highest honors are paid to men of sterling principle, and so it will always be since God rules.

Integrity is not merely honesty of action, but honesty of intention. It is an innate quality of the mind and heart.

It is one of the greatest elements in an eminently successful life.

NOVEMBER TWENTY-THREE

Learn to Live Well and Nobly

It is better to have success late in life than not at all. You must respect yourself if you want others to respect you. It is a valuable habit to keep the little moments filled with big work.

The best way to lose your sorrow is to sympathize with others. There are no dull hours for the man who looks only on the bright side of life. Keep interested and you will draw interest.

Let the encyclopedia carry the load of details so that you can use your mind principally for original thinking. It is a good rule never to borrow from a friend, and better still not to borrow from any one.

The troubles you think may come next month will probably be as remote then as they are now.

Spend your time in being what you are, not in trying to appear what you are not.

NOVEMBER TWENTY-FOUR

Cultivate Fineness of Character

Seemingly small things have large consequences.

A foolish slip of speech, an empty laugh, an ungainly position, un unkind or irrelevant remark, an unpleasant mannerism, or an undignified habit, may unconsciously lower you in the estimation of others.

Life is made up largely of trifles. To win and retain the esteem of your fellow men you must be discriminating in your thoughts and actions.

Culture demands constant alertness. Be on strict guard against undesirable habits which would injure you in the eyes of other men.

If you now have any such habits, take radical and prompt means to correct them.

Begin by making a written list today of the things you wish to eradicate from your personal character.

NOVEMBER TWENTY-FIVE

How to Produce the Best Results

There are times when it is best for you to keep still, and to let the solution of your problem find its own way into your mind. Great achievement does not depend upon ceaseless activity.

The time you give to quiet meditation, to play of the imagination, and to mental planning, may vitally contribute to subsequent accomplishment.

It is not always the busiest man who produces the greatest results.

Men of wide experience recognize the value of poise, deliberateness, and self-restraint. It is highly beneficial to cultivate the habit of getting things done without haste, anxiety, nor impulsiveness.

These faculties of your mind best discharge their function when you are in a state of quiet confidence.

NOVEMBER TWENTY-SIX

Build Well and Strongly Today

You can constantly find in others something good to praise and endorse. Look for the best, the bright, the beautiful all about you.

Make your thought constructive and progressive. Build well and strongly day by day, knowing that multiplied right thoughts yield inevitably right results. The habit of generous and appreciative praise of others will give you a mental uplift.

There is innate satisfaction in looking for the true and the noble. Men who are known always to speak well of others are in great favor.

Strict adherence to the rule never to speak ill of any one will save you from many bitter experiences and regrets.

Your silent estimate of others profoundly affects their lives and yours.

If you would make men praiseworthy, praise them.

NOVEMBER TWENTY-SEVEN

There is a Large Life for You

Force of will is not sufficient to rid you of such tenacious faults as anger, worry, fear, and discontent. Your remedy is to substitute superior thoughts.

Set before yourself a great life purpose, regularly substitute harmony for anger, peace for worry, confidence for fear, and agreeableness for discontent.

As the expulsive power of right ideas becomes clear to you, desirable habits will easily be made to take the place of old ones.

Open your mind and heart to great and noble thoughts, and your character will assume new strength and significance. The remedy for your faults is not repression, but substitution.

Live daily upon an exalted mental plane, and there will come to your constantly increasing opportunities.

INSPIRATION AND IDEALS

NOVEMBER TWENTY-EIGHT

The Purpose of Good Resolutions

It is comparatively easy to live up to your resolutions until the unexpected happens. Then they are put to a severe test.

The strength of your resolutions is possibly strained to the extreme limit, but if they are properly rooted you will emerge victorious.

The value of a fulfilled resolution is that it encourages you to make still better and stronger resolutions.

The object of making a resolution is the obviate repetition of a mistake, or to improve your way of doing things.

When you fully realize the value of this self-discipline, you will apply it as often as you discover the need for it in your character and daily life.

Resolutions are essential to real progress, and there can be no great achievement without them.

NOVEMBER TWENTY-NINE

Render Real Service to Others

The truest service you can render is that which you do quietly and silently, and without expectation of gratitude or reward.

Do not wait for special occasions, but serve today as opportunity offers. Say the kind and encouraging word. Send a bright and helpful letter to an absent friend.

Distribute a few copies of an inspiring book where they will do the most good. Render a special service to one less fortunate than yourself. Send some flowers to a sick or discouraged friend.

When the spirit is willing, many suggestions will occur to you whereby you can radiate sunshine along the daily pathway of life.

Where true gentleness is and desire for service, there you will find greatness of heart and sincere love of God.

NOVEMBER THIRTY

Plan, Work, Pray, and Serve

Your life should consist chiefly of work, service, cooperation, achievement, and happiness. An intelligently planned world would have no room nor provision for sin, sickness, discord, worry, fear nor other ills which affect mankind.

These man-made beliefs will be eliminated as rapidly as men conform their lives to God's truth and law.

\The world steadily advances toward a glorious goal, and you can do your share to speed its progress by keeping your personal life in harmony with the divine plan.

Give a portion of your time daily to prayer, meditation, and spiritual culture.

Read each day the thoughts of some great religious writer, that they may quicken you.

Keep your life strong, true, purposeful, and Godward.

DECEMBER

DECEMBER ONE

Grow Daily in Power and Purpose

The giant tree tells an inspiring and instructive story of growth, beauty, and usefulness. Straight and dignified, it speaks of sturdiness and serenity in storm and sunshine.

Its roots symbolize depth and security. Its graceful leaves and branches are expressions of harmony and beauty.

Silent and supreme, it serves as sentinel, shade, and shelter.

The growth and unfolding of your life should be as beautiful and progressive as that of the giant tree.

Let your character be firmly rooted in principle, your mind set constantly toward the light, and your aims and aspirations point heavenward.

Then, like the giant tree, you will steadily grow in beauty and power, inspiring men about you, and fulfilling the divine purpose.

DECEMBER TWO

Study Truth and Righteousness

Life is worthwhile if you are growing daily in spiritual power and purpose.

Life is worthwhile if you are constantly unfolding in beauty and nobility of character. Life is worth while if you are daily rendering useful service to others.

Life is worthwhile if you are meeting every responsibility, obligation, and circumstance with confidence and unwavering faith.

Life is worthwhile if you are progessing in truth and righteousness.

Life is worthwhile if despite the sin, sickness, and sorrow of the world you still keep radiant and strong.

Life is transcendently worth while if you are daily developing a deep consciousness of your personal alliance with God, your dependence upon Him, and the absolute assurance of His guidance and protection.

DECEMBER THREE

Take a Definite Stand Today

A serious responsibility rests upon you not only to use the talents you have, but to multiply them into more talents.

Service to God implies a life of daily progression. It is your paramount business to grow daily in good works, strong through prayer.

The right use of your talents and opportunities is a form of divine service, since right is good, and all good is of God.

The abilities you possess are a priceless gift, and your gratitude will best be shown by the way you use these great powers.

Take a definite stand today for a larger and more useful life, resolve to put your superior talents to the best use, and be assured that reward and recognition await you.

DECEMBER FOUR

The Vital Elements of Good Health

Good health depends primarily upon right thinking and consequent right habits of life.

Vigilantly guard your mind against erroneous and destructive thought, as you would guard your house against burglars and assassins. A beneficent power cooperates with you when you engage in right thinking.

To be thoroughly well, you must be thoroughly good, and goodness is primarily of the mind and heart. Harmonious thinking strengthens, stimulates, and nourishes the body.

Cheerfulness, purity, and righteousness are vital elements of good health. The rewards of virtue are certain, immediate, and satisfying. Hold tenaciously to the principles of truth, honor, and justice.

Right thinking is a great creative force with which to build a healthy and beautiful life.

DECEMBER FIVE

Grow in Vitality and Power

A man given up at forty to die, lived to be over a hundred years old, due to the two habits of temperance and regularity.

He resolved to make these cardinal rules of his life, and so applied them to his eating, sleeping, exercise, and daily activities.

Steadily he grew in strength, and at a period when most men think of passing on, he was planning new interests with which to keep his mind occupied.

As you develop and apply these habits of temperance and regularity, you will grow in vitality and power.

Your mind will assume new force and clearness, and you will have a sense of larger purpose and usefulness in the world.

These rules of temperance and regularity should be applied to all things in order to achieve the highest results.

DECEMBER SIX

Realize Your Superior Endowments

It is one of your paramount duties to develop in yourself proper sense of personal worth and dignity. Honorable self-respect is a prerequisite to large influence and success.

There is a laudable price which you will do well to cultivate, in order to occupy your rightful position in the world.

As you develop your personal qualities of excellence, honor, self-esteem, independence, you will more fully live and express the life for which you were intended.

There is a larger life for you than you are now living, vastly greater purpose than you have yet attained.

The more fully you realize your superior personal endowments, the more you will wish to realize the ideal life which God has made possible to you.

DECEMBER SEVEN

Develop Power Through Repose

Give yourself up occasionally to thorough relaxation.

Drop all tension of the arms, legs and neck. Stop all nervous habits such as tapping with the hands and feet, twitching the mouth or eyes, and constantly moving from one position to another.

Take little opportunities to rest your nerves. Occasionally close your eyes when riding on a train or street-car.

Learn to let go. Develop power through repose. Rest is as necessary as labor. By means of proper rest and relaxation you will return to your work with clearer brain and increased vitality.

Save yourself from little tiresome acts by working in poise. Give your powers free play, but do not be over-anxious about results.

Results are in the hands of God.

DECEMBER EIGHT

Keep Your Mental Plane High

Your character will be as high as your plane of consciousness.

Think rightly and greatly, and your life will be an expression of this high standard. It is the spiritual and mental law.

You gain something from every good, beautiful, and true thought which you receive into your mind.

The full worth, meaning, and possibility of your life can become manifest only through elevation and purification of thought.

As you nourish your mind upon supreme ideals, you will steadily rise in the scale of human values, and there will one day come to you a satisfying realization that God has indeed given you all things to possess in the proportion that you have been a willing disciple of His truth.

DECEMBER NINE

Be Still and Learn God

Plan a daily period of at least ten minutes when you can be alone for quiet, deep, meditative thinking. This is essential to your best mental growth.

In social intercourse you are constantly drawing upon your mental resources, but it is equally important that you have times of silence and solitude for concentrated, original, profound thinking.

Your mind does not yield up its richest treasures while you are busily occupied with varied aims and interests.

It is when you grow still and there are no distracting influences at work, that your most valuable thoughts disclose themselves.

Ascertain what is your best time for clear and original thinking, whether the early morning or the late evening, then reserve a regular period for this vital work.

DECEMBER TEN

Good Thoughts Yield Good Results

It is in your power to make this day one of the best and brightest of days.

Begin with an inspiring thought and a deep desire to make the most of your present opportunities.

As you sow good thoughts you will reap good results.

Open the windows of your mind and let in the sunshine of good cheer, optimism, and generous good will.

A right mental attitude will help you and others with whom you come in contact to live well and happily.

Make this day bright and productive by filling it with ambitious and purposeful work. Look only for the good and you will find the good.

The mental power which you now possess will grow still greater in the process of right use, and each day can be better and brighter than ever before.

DECEMBER ELEVEN

Cultivate Personal Poise

True poise is spiritual in basis. There is an ease of manner which arises from serenity of mind, but this is not the highest kind of poise.

Many persons are said to be in poise when they are only relaxed or indifferent.

Poise is an inner property of the soul. It is power in reserve and repose. It is self-possession born of experience and fine discrimination.

Poise of this type is the outcome of personal rectitude and clear-sighted common sense.

It is evidence that a man has come to himself and is in the realization and enjoyment of his best powers.

Such poise is worthy of most careful cultivation, since it implies possession of those sterling qualities which invariably characterize the highly successful man.

DECEMBER TWELVE

Rightly Estimate Your Abilities

Self-approbation is a subtle foe to progress. Men who flatter and eulogize you most may be rendering you the least service.

The natural inclination to excuse to yourself your own errors is a serious hindrance to growth in sound judgment.

Men who are fickle, vacillating, and faint-hearted do not win honor and distinction in the great race of life. The race is not to the swift only, but to the brave, intelligent and efficient.

While it is well for you to have full confidence in your powers and possibilities, deeming nothing within reason too high for your aspiration, you should know how to appraise your personal resources accurately.

A right estimate of your abilities will contribute materially to your progress toward a useful and successful life.

DECEMBER THIRTEEN

The Foundation of Success

Your personal success largely depends upon the degree to which you develop and use the following cardinal qualities:

Accuracy, adaptability, alertness, ambition, concentration, confidence, courage, courtesy, decision, determination, diligence, discretion, earnestness, economy, efficiency, enthusiasm, faith, foresight, honesty, independence, industry, initiative, integrity, judgment, loyalty, nobility, optimism, orderliness, patience, persistence, precision, promptness, prudence, punctuality, purpose, reliability, resourcefulness, self-control, sincerity, stamina, sympathy, tact, temperance, tenacity, thoroughness, thrift, truthfulness, vigilance, vigor, zeal.

Develop and use qualities daily.

DECEMBER FOURTEEN

Make Use of Divine Truth

To every problem there is already a solution, whether you know it or not.

To every sum in mathematics there is already a correct answer, whether the mathematician has found it or not.

Correct answers to all mathematical problems have always existed, and therefore while you may discover the right answers you cannot possibly create them.

It is obvious from this that your principal work in the pursuit of any branch of knowledge is not so much as to create, as to recognize, realize, and appropriate.

It should be encouraging to you to know that if you are now confronted by any kind of problem, personal or otherwise, there is a way to solve it, and you will find the way as rapidly and as surely as you apply to it the principles of divine truth.

DECEMBER FIFTEEN

Gentleness is True Power

Kindness wins where coercion fails. Sympathy smooths out the difficulties and disarms antagonism. The supreme qualities of kindness and gentleness can be rapidly cultivated by close attention to the little things. They grow through use.

It is erroneous to think of gentleness as necessarily weak and timid. In the truest sense gentleness is power and poise. It is positive virtue reaching out to understand, help, and encourage. It is eloquent evidence of nobility of soul.

Sympathy and gentleness are safeguards against selfishness.

Three valuable personal qualities are kindness, gentleness, and sympathy.

The time you devote to cultivating these virtues will give breadth to your character, and help to shape your life towards noble ends.

DECEMBER SIXTEEN

Diligently Work and You Will Win

The men who have accomplished great things in the world have invariably been prodigious workers. You will do well to emulate their example.

Whatever your present responsibilities are, apply yourself to them with diligence. Purpose and endurance are the handmaids of successful enterprise.

Many men have the means but not the application for great achievement. The one certain way to win distinction in any line of endeavor is through intelligent and incessant labor.

The records of highly successful men are open to you for your guidance and inspiration.

Above all things else they counsel you to work if you would win.

The price of real attainment is an indomitable will to persevere under all circumstances.

DECEMBER SEVENTEEN

Health, Harmony, and Happiness

Your mind is a field, a garden, a storehouse, a communications hub, a clearing house.

It will keep you fully occupied to cultivate this field and garden, to store up golden truths in the recesses of your memory, to send out uplifting thoughts to others, and to keep this wonderful mental world of yours in order.

All that is really worth while in your life is first outlined in your mind. Ideas and ideals, plans and purposes, aims and aspirations, all begin there.

Let your mental workshop claim your constant attention.

Remember that good thoughts carry the essence of health, harmony, and happiness.

All of God's laws are laws of love, truth, and justice.

Let these laws forever rule your mind and life.

DECEMBER EIGHTEEN

Study Truth for Truth's Sake

The vital step to the apprehension of truth is to desire it sincerely and earnestly. To make truth wholly yours, you must both understand and practically apply it.

You will better appreciate the value and importance of truth when you seriously consider that erroneous thinking is the chief cause of all the sin, disaster, misfortune, sickness, and failure in the world.

Truth to be properly grasped must be studied for truth's sake.

Truth to be of real significance to you must be something more than theory; it must be vital, personal, demonstrated power in your daily life.

There is nothing which will bring to you so much satisfaction and permanent benefit as a profound study of truth. It transcends all material possessions, since it is eternal.

DECEMBER NINETEEN

You Are What You Are

Your personal appearance is an asset of great importance. The world's first appraisal of you is your outward personality.

What you wear is an expression of what you are. A discriminating mind manifests itself in countless little ways. Your attire, attitude, and manner proclaim you to others. Your appearance announces you before you speak.

Realize the vital importance of always appearing at your best. When you so appear it will increase your self-respect, and help to win the good opinion of others.

You are what you are. No masquerading in assumed manners, no lofty pretentiousness, no mere conforming to social custom will make you more than you are.

True worth is of the mind and heart.

Culture and character are intrinsic.

DECEMBER TWENTY

Apply Your Heart to Wisdom

Beware prejudice. It closes the door to truth and knowledge. It is a subtle foe to mental growth and progress.

Prejudice is a prolific cause of harsh and unsound opinions.

The best way to clarify your ideas, and to verify your judgments, is to bring them into conflict with other minds.

It is a good thing to believe you can learn something from every one you meet. It is more profitable for you to look for faults in your own judgment than in that of others.

It is of prime importance that you put your own mind in order before undertaking to set other people aright.

Wisdom is the power of true and just discernment.

Solomon says that man is happy who finds it. Therefore apply your heart diligently to wisdom.

DECEMBER TWENTY-ONE

The Power and Majesty of Winter

Beautiful winter! Kind of seasons, majestic ruler of the year. Stern, strong, sublime, you summon men to action and achievement.

You stir their blood and bid them work and win.

Over the wide earth you cast your mantle of white, converting it into a place of fairy enchantment.

Your silver snows, sparking and radiant in the sunlight, have taken the place of summer-scented flowers.

It is the time of happy firesides, intimate friendships, long evenings, and significant silences – dream-time as well as work-time.

Glorious winter! – imparting to life richness and vitality.

Beautiful, invigorating, inspiring winter! – symbol of purity, grandeur, and power.

DECEMBER TWENTY-TWO

The Best is Available to You

The best things are not remote and inaccessible. They are near you, within your grasp, and ever available.

The best times are not in the dim future, but here and now in the living present. The best opportunities are not reserved in some distant place, but are within your reach right where you are today.

Heaven is not tucked away in some indefinite place in the sky, but is within you. All that is good and fine and noble in life is now available to you.

You will no longer suffer from self-limitation, doubt, and discouragement, once you have fully realized how much has been provided for you.

Today earnestly resolve to claim these priceless gifts and opportunities and to use them for your largest unfoldment.

DECEMBER TWENTY-THREE

Cultivate a Helpful Hobby

However absorbing and pleasurable your regular occupation may be, you should also have a hobby to which you can turn for change and recuperation.

The brain and body weary of repeated effort. The man of one idea eventually pays a penalty disproportionate to the results.

There are many delightful hobbies, such as gardening, music, languages, handicraft, sketching, nature studies, and writing, which will give new purpose and vitality to your daily work.

The happiest man is he who, as the years advance, finds continued interest in a variety of subjects, and who has a particular hobby for change and relaxation.

You are fortunate if you are engaged in congenial work, but you are doubly so if you have an interesting hobby.

DECEMBER TWENTY-FOUR

As You Climb the Heights

There is inexpressible joy in the realization of having completely conquered a secret weakness, successfully solved a formidable problem, or faithfully discharged a disagreeable duty.

To many life is like climbing a long, steep, difficult hill; but as the years pass, those who courageously press on and up find themselves at last upon the mountain top of achievement, where they look out upon a scene of indescribable beauty, and, as they turn to look back and down at the road they have traversed, perhaps rough and difficult in many places, they realize that it has all been worth-while, and that the final reward of work well done has fully compensated them for the effort.

Life is a beautiful and inspiring journey for the courageous traveler.

DECEMBER TWENTY-FIVE

The Season and Spirit of Service

The Christmas spirit and sense of service should not be only for one day in the year, but a perennial and perpetual expression of the love in your heart.

If the spiritual good cheer of Christmas Day were generally manifested throughout the year it would transform mankind.

Love is still the greatest thing in the world, and the world grows better in proportion that love increases.

Do not wait for others to practice the golden rule, but diligently apply it in your own daily life.

Like the stars that are beautiful because of what they are, and not because of what they do, so you can make your life a beneficent influence to others by developing a continual spirit of Christmas within your mind and heart.

DECEMBER TWENTY-SIX

The Values and Rewards of Life

Mellowness, contentment, and repose should mark the advancing years of a well-planned life.

It is characteristic of your to be alert, expectant, and energetic, but as one advances along the pathway of life, experience and knowledge should bring a sense of inner peace, power, and confidence.

The lessons of life are intended to confer the ability to secure right results without undue haste.

In later years when there comes a deep realization of life's values and rewards, one should listen and meditate much, because only through quietness it is possible to come into intimate touch with the spiritual.

Thus may life be beautifully rounded out into fullness, and one may then wait with confidence for the sweet benediction of God.

DECEMBER TWENTY-SEVEN

Advancing Along Life's Pathway

Elderly people should never say, "I'm too old," "My day is past," "Once I was young," "If I could only life my life over," "There is no use of trying now," "Only young people are wanted," "I'm tired of living," "It isn't worth the struggle," "I feel I'm in the way," "I should have made more friends," "I am no use now," "I missed my chance," "I'm ready to go any time," "I married too soon," "I was too generous," "I'm through with the world," "The end is not far off," "I'll welcome death," "I hope I'll go soon," "Anything is good enough for me now," "Be sure not to bury me alive."

This is wrong and destructive.

Life should graduate gracefully from ardent youth to superb old age, and from that to later golden years with God's blessing overhead.

DECEMBER TWENTY-EIGHT

Refining Influences of Life

Culture is that form of education which manifests itself in refinement of mind, morals, and taste.

Once evidence of culture is to have the courage to be what you are. Culture includes not only knowledge, but sympathy and intelligence.

Culture combines simplicity and courtesy. Culture is the growth of all the graces of love, beauty, truth, and service, and the repression of everything mean or unworthy.

Culture expels evil with good, ignorance with knowledge and falsity with truth.

Culture practices the small humanities, abhors uncleanness of every kind, and has an innate desire to do the right thing.

Culture unfolds the refining influence of life, and clearns the way for those who would follow toward the light.

DECEMBER TWENTY-NINE

Be True to Your Highest Self

Serve and trust God. Keep his commandments.

Work out your own salvation with fear and trembling. Glorify God in your body, and in your spirit, which are His.

Fight the good fight of faith.

Let the word of Christ dwell in you richly in all wisdom. Let no corrupt communication proceed out of your mouth, but that which is good to the use of edifying.

Keep your heart with all diligence, for out of it are the issues of life. Be renewed in the spirit of your mind; and put on the new man, which after God is created in righteousness and true holiness. Responsibility precedes reward.

Do your part faithfully, that you may be worthy of the crown of righteousness promised to those who are obedient.

You are the temple of the living God.

DECEMBER THIRTY

Keep Your Record Clean

Your life is like a book. The title-page is your name. The preface is your introduction to the world.

The pages are a daily chronicle of your efforts, trials, pleasures, discouragements, ambitions, and achievements.

The principle subject of your book may be business, romance, tragedy, comedy, poetry, science, literature, or religion.

Day by day your thoughts and acts are being inscribed as evidence of your success or failure. What you will record on the remaining pages of your book is of vital importance.

Hour by hour the record is being made which must stand for all time. One day the word "Finis" must be written.

Let it be said of your book that it is a record of noble purpose, generous service, and work well done.

DECEMBER THIRTY-ONE

Make Still Better Plans

At the closing of the old year, you can profitably make an inventory of what you have planned, developed, and achieved.

Carefully consider the means and methods which you have used for desired ends, and the special instances in which you have succeeded or failed.

As you look in retrospect, you will doubtless see many places where better judgment, broader clarity, and greater prudence could have been used by you with more satisfactory results.

So while you think with gratitude and pleasure of the progress you have made and the results achieved, take a practical lesson from such personal examination, and earnestly resolve to make the new year a better, bigger, brighter one for yourself and for the world in which you live.

About Philippa Burgess

Working as a professional in Marketing, PR and Creative Project Management, Philippa Burgess has inspired and brought to life countless projects. As a transplant from New York City, she moved to Los Angeles when Hollywood beckoned where she attended the University of Southern California (USC). Upon graduation she landed at a major Hollywood talent agency in the motion picture literary department and then went on to work in literary management and marketing in the entertainment industry.

The Rocky Mountains of Colorado are now home, where she focuses on inspiring others to tell their stories through both traditional and digital media.

Philippa is a member of the TV Academy (Emmys®) and AuthorU.org. She is currently working to earn her 3rd degree black belt in Shaolin Kung Fu.

Philippa Burgess is available for speaking and consultation for organizations and conferences. You can learn more and connect with her through her websites:

InspirationandIdeals.com
PhilippaBurgess.com

Connect and Follow her at:

PhilippaAuthor

PhilippaBurgess

InspiringIdeals

PhilippaBurgess

PhilippaBurgess

AKNOWLEDGMENTS

This book was inspired by Grenville Kleiser's *Inspiration and Ideals: Thoughts for Every Day* (1917). Grenville Kleiser wrote and dedicated it in New York City. The original copy of the book that I own contains the signature of a Robert Earle McCarty and the year 1938 penned on the inside of the back cover. According to the 1940 census, McCarty was 20 years old at that time and living in Los Angeles, having lived in Denver, Colorado prior to that. From East Coast to West Coast to the Rocky Mountains, I seem to have covered some of the same ground as these two gentlemen.

I also wish to acknowledge my mom, Madeline Burgess, my parents Peter Burgess and Dawn Beverley, my siblings Brendan Burgess and Shivonne Beverley, and a huge and great extended family.

To my pastors, teachers and peers at St. Cassian's in Upper Montclair, New Jersey; The Church of the Heavenly Rest in New York City; Westwood Presbyterian Church in Los Angeles; Rosicrucian Fellowship in Oceanside, California; University of Southern California (USC); St. Andrews Episcopal Church in Denver; and the Chinese Shaolin Center for Kung Fu, Tai Chi & Wooden Man in Los Angeles and Denver; David Palmer: The Leo King; and all the people and places where I got education, training and spiritual instruction.

To my colleagues and friends at Author U.org, with my greatest thanks to Dr. Judith Briles and everyone on my publishing team including Nick Zelinger, Jeanne Stratton, Joel Hinrichs, Bobby Crew, and Ashlee Bratton.

Inspiration and Ideals

To my friends and colleagues in CAI-RMC (Community Associations Institute – Rocky Mountain Chapter), SMPS Colorado (Society of Marketing Professional Services), Television Academy and Television Academy, Interactive Media Peer Group, RVC (Rockies Venture Club), (MJBA) Marijuana Business Association, Colorado Creative Industries, and The University Club of Denver.

To Brent Rumpf, David Gray, Stan Wagner, Robert "Sonny" Wiegand II, Michael Conti, Rhondda Hartman, Tom Fielding, Jeanne Fielding, Steve Murray, Wendi Medved, Gwen Miller, Wes Wollenweber, Honnie Korngold and Larry Douglas for keeping me gainfully employed in Colorado.

To everyone else in my life who knows me and who has been there to cheerlead me (you know who you are) with a special shout out to Lisa Shepard Reid, Craig Reid, Brad Kushner, Shannon McMahon, Mark Knight, Jett Knight, Christina Azharian, Linda Frothingham, Tom Kramis, and Catherine Carilli.

I'm grateful to you all.

Philippa

GIVE THE GIFT OF
INSPIRATION AND IDEALS
TO YOUR FRIENDS AND COLLEAGUES

YES, I want _____ copies of *Inspiration and Ideals: Thoughts for Every Day*

YES, I am interested in having Philippa Burgess speak to my company, association, school, or organization. Please send me information.

Include $6 for shipping and handling for one book, and $2.50 for each additional book. Colorado, Ohio and New York residents must include applicable sales tax. Canadian or other foreign orders must include payment in US funds with 7% GST added.

Payment must accompany orders. Allow 3 weeks for delivery.

My check or money order of $_____ is enclosed.

Please charge my   Visa   MasterCard   American Express   Discover

Name_____

Organization_____

Address_____

City/State/Zip_____

Phone_____ Email_____

Card #_____

Exp.Date_____ CVV code_____

Signature_____

Make your check payable and return to:
Inspiration & Ideals LLC
9975 Wadsworth Pkwy
Unit K2,
Westminster, CO 80021
(720) 608-6201
Or, go to
www.InspirationandIdeals.com

INDEX OF SUBJECTS

Abilities	46	Breathing	98
Abundance	269	Broadmindedness	85
Accomplishment	275	Brotherhood	90
Achievement	207	Capacity	226
Acquisition	65	Carriage	196
Adaptability	109	Character	121
Admonition	228	Characteristics	128
Advancement	263	Charm	203
Advice	335	Cheerfulness	211
Affirmation	248	Choice	337
Age	393	Christmas	391
Aims	5	Common Sense	258
Alertness	247	Composure	358
Alliance	178	Concentration	56
Ambition	250	Conditions	23
Amenability	18	Confidence	83
Anger	320	Confusion	150
Annoyances	220	Conscientiousness	80
Appearance	385	Consecration	395
Application	78	Consequences	356
Appraisement	329	Conservation	206
Appreciation	323	Considerateness	192
Appropriation	172	Constructiveness	159
Approval	60	Contentment	342
Aspiration	264	Contrasts	9
Assets	181	Conversation	63
Assurance	187	Convictions	170
Attractiveness	276	Cooperation	301
Auto-suggestion	151	Counsel	173
Autumn	291	Courage	330
Availability	388	Criticism	49
Bathing	238	Culture	394
Beauty	193	Decision	6
Beginning	3	Dedication	45
Beliefs	177	Deeds	97
Birthright	343	Defects	129
Books	198	Deficiencies	127

Definiteness	93	Example	215
Deliberateness	174	Exclusiveness	114
Delusion	285	Exercise	139
Dependence	213	Expectation	74
Depression	155	Experience	58
Desires	218	Expression	260
Determination	81	Failure	106
Development	379	Fairness	231
Devotion	51	Faith	325
Difficulties	146	Fastidiousness	17
Dignity	349	Faults	96
Diligence	210	Felicity	289
Direction	312	Fidelity	255
Discernment	386	Fineness	283
Discipleship	346	Flexibility	70
Discipline	245	Flowers	201
Discord	202	Foresight	230
Discouragement	195	Foundations	117
Distinction	103	Freedom	144
Doing	243	Friendship	89
Duty	115	Fruitage	383
Earnestness	310	Fulfillment	48
Education	280	Fundamentals	298
Effects	122	Generosity	235
Effort	28	Geniality	293
Elimination	24	Genuineness	282
Eloquence	302	Giving	216
Emergencies	222	Gladness	194
Eminence	236	God	183
Emulation	112	Godwardness	364
Endowment	38	Good-will	376
Endurance	382	Goodness	82
Energy	31	Gratitude	242
Enjoyment	350	Greatness	104
Enrichment	94	Growth	161
Enterprise	14	Guidance	15
Enthusiasm	270	Habits	204
Essentials	123	Handicaps	288
Evil	322	Happiness	126
Exaltation	71	Harmony	272

Index of Subjects

Haste	57	Loyalty	317
Health	370	Majesty	239
Helpfulness	287	Manners	40
Heritage	148	Mastery	292
Hindrances	378	Mastication	72
Hobbies	389	Maturity	315
Holiness	309	Mediocrity	308
Honesty	99	Meditation	125
Horizons	254	Mellowness	392
Humility	138	Mentality	160
Ideals	347	Mercies	27
Idleness	156	Merit	279
Ignorance	278	Mind	171
Impressions	212	Mistakes	175
Improvement	76	Money	294
Imprudence	147	Motives	169
Indecision	157	Nobility	118
Independence	21	Non-resistance	241
Industry	209	Obstacles	345
Influence	132	Occupation	140
Initiative	162	Omissions	246
Inspiration	348	Onwardness	355
Integrity	354	Opinions	253
Intention	277	Opportunity	185
Interests	30	Opposition	197
Interruptions	59	Optimism	37
Intimations	12	Order	256
Intuition	137	Originality	328
Joyousness	327	Overcoming	390
Judgment	20	Patience	286
Kindness	381	Peace	64
Knowledge	142	People	225
Labor	319	Perfection	321
Life	368	Performance	262
Light	16	Perseverance	119
Listening	214	Persistence	224
Literature	259	Personality	92
Longing	22	Perspective	353
Loquacity	257	Petition	273
Love	7	Plans	111

Poise	303	Rest	373
Possession	33	Results	229
Possibilities	163	Retrospect	397
Posture	306	Riches	26
Power	95	Righteousness	307
Practice	43	Satisfaction	29
Praise	359	Schooling	360
Prayer	336	Scripture	110
Prejudice	357	Sculptors	19
Preparation	290	Sea, The	311
Principle	145	Selectiveness	249
Problems	281	Self-confidence	141
Procrastination	190	Self-control	208
Progress	227	Self-discipline	107
Promise	73	Self-examination	158
Provision	221	Self-government	331
Prudence	135	Self-limitation	42
Purpose	314	Self-possession	377
Qualities	186	Self-reliance	324
Questions	47	Self-surrender	61
Quietness	124	Serenity	182
Reading	339	Service	363
Realization	313	Shortcomings	149
Receptivity	244	Silence	179
Reciprocity	8	Simplicity	131
Record	396	Sin	136
Refinement	25	Sincerity	261
Reflection	13	Sky, The	265
Reformation	120	Smiling	341
Regrets	295	Solicitude	108
Reinforcement	75	Solitude	11
Reiteration	10	Solutions	380
Relaxation	130	Speech	84
Religion	223	Spirituality	304
Repetition	205	Spring	88
Repose	274	Stability	362
Resistance	39	Standard	340
Resolutions	252	Stillness	113
Resources	143	Stocktaking	176
Responsibility	326	Study	318

Index of Subjects

Submission	297	Truth	384
Substitution	153	Unfoldment	375
Success	284	Universal Law	4
Suggestions	352	Upbuilding	77
Summer	189	Usefulness	316
Supply	338	Values	344
Supremacy	374	Variety	240
Symbols	55	Verbosity	164
System	154	Vigilance	191
Talents	369	Vigor	69
Talking	105	Vision	237
Taste	251	Vitality	188
Temperance	371	Walking	50
Tests	351	Waste	52
Thoroughness	44	Water	180
Thought	361	Welfare	41
Thoughts	296	Wholeness	32
Time	87	Will	53
Today	62	Winter	387
Tolerance	116	Wisdom	271
Tranquility	219	Words	86
Trees	367	Work	79
Trials	217	Worry	184
Trifles	165	Worth	372
Troubles	54	Writing	91
Trust	152	Zeal	305